The Rain Garden Planner

SEVEN STEPS TO CONSERVING AND MANAGING WATER IN THE GARDEN

Terry Wallace

4880 Lower Valley Road · Atglen, PA 19310

Schiffer Books are available at special discounts for bulk purchases for sales promotions or premiums. Special editions, including personalized covers, corporate imprints, and excerpts can be created in large quantities for special needs. For more information contact the publisher:

Published by Schiffer Publishing Ltd.
4880 Lower Valley Road
Atglen, PA 19310
Phone: (610) 593-1777; Fax: (610) 593-2002
E-mail: Info@schifferbooks.com

For the largest selection of fine reference books on this and related subjects, please visit our web site at **www.schifferbooks.com**
We are always looking for people to write books on new and related subjects. If you have an idea for a book please contact us at the above address.

This book may be purchased from the publisher.
Include $5.00 for shipping.
Please try your bookstore first.
You may write for a free catalog.

In Europe, Schiffer books are distributed by
Bushwood Books
6 Marksbury Ave.
Kew Gardens
Surrey TW9 4JF England
Phone: 44 (0) 20 8392-8585; Fax: 44 (0) 20 8392-9876
E-mail: info@bushwoodbooks.co.uk
Website: www.bushwoodbooks.co.uk
Free postage in the U.K., Europe; air mail at cost.

Designed by RoS
Type set in Esperanza/Zurich BT

ISBN: 978-0-7643-3116-9
Printed in China

Acknowledgements

Many people have contributed to this book. Where to start? The senior landscape architects of Wallace Associates, especially Laura Miller, were early advocates of Rain Gardens and sustainable landscaping. They sparked an interest in water conserving gardens that led me to the writing of this book. Many of the illustrations in this text are photos of gardens they designed. Thank you Richard Lyon, Laura Miller, and Tim Peterson.

At Temple University I was inspired and informed by Jenny Rose Carey. As Director of the Landscape Arboretum at Temple's Ambler, Pennsylvania, campus, she took time out of a very busy schedule to help me understand Temple's Sustainable Wetland Garden and wetland gardens in general. She also generously allowed me to photograph "Northview," her imaginative personal garden. Temple Associates Ann Marie Rambo, Rudy Keller, and Pauline Hurley-Kurtz each contributed to my knowledge of what it takes to create a rain garden that is "As attractive to people as it is to wildlife." All of these people are hands-on gardeners that we encountered as Ms. Carey and I toured the grounds. I particularly valued their insights since my intention was to write a guide for people who enjoy doing their gardening themselves.

Kelly Gutshall of Land Studies Inc. in Lititz, Pennsylvania, generously spent hours showing and explaining the important work her firm is doing in flood plain restoration and sustainable landscaping. She added considerably to my understanding of natural wetlands and water cycles as well as flood control measures and habitat restoration.

Many others have contributed with their knowledge, encouragement, and inspiration. Thanks to all of you.

Table of Contents

Introduction
The Value of Water

"Water is the most basic of all resources. Civilizations grew or withered depending on its availability."

Dr. Nathan W. Snyder,
Ralph M. Parsons Engineering

What is clear, tasteless, readily available, inexpensive, and absolutely essential to all life on earth? It's water of course. In our day-to-day lives we don't give a lot of thought to water. It may seem to be a basic right to many of us—like the air we breath. After all, we turn on the tap and clean, fresh water pours forth in a seemingly endless supply. Global warming, endangered species, rising fuel prices, slowing economies—we have enough to worry about. Water may seem to be the least of our concerns.

Consider for a moment what it would mean for your life if you turned the tap and no water issued forth. As the earth becomes more heavily populated, and its inhabitants demand increasingly high standards of living, pressure on all resources has grown dramatically. In much of the United States there is a plentiful water supply. That may be altered as our changing climate produces increasingly severe cycles of drought and flooding.

Why should individuals be concerned? Isn't this a problem for municipalities to address? Yes and no. Municipalities are not likely to help when your basement is flooded or your lawn remains soggy for months at a time. Municipal authorities might warn you to evacuate or rescue you when floodwater laps at your doorstep, but they can't restore your lost valuables. And there is little municipal authorities can do when there is an extended drought and water supplies dry up. Without our help and cooperation, water problems could overwhelm local and national government efforts in the foreseeable future.

A wet mesic meadow conserves and cleanses water. It is a component of the hydrologic cycle.

Natural wetlands such as this play an important role in the storage of water and flood prevention. Credit: LandStudies Inc.

There is much we can do to manage our resources so that we continue to enjoy a high standard of living. This book details some simple and practical methods for homeowners to help conserve our clean and plentiful water supply. The main subject is the rain garden, an effective water filtration and conservation system that is within the reach of most of us. The chapters of this book contain all the details for designing, installing and maintaining a rain garden along with what to expect and some of the pitfalls. I have also included a chapter on other ways of conserving and protecting our clean water supply and a long list of resources for learning more about water, its importance to us and conservation practices. My hope is that this book, written to appeal to a wide audience, inspires many individuals to do a little more to improve water management. If we all make the effort our children and grandchildren can look forward to the continued benefits of a sparkling, healthy, and plentiful water supply.

Small rain gardens such as this parking lot island, are very effective at filtering pollutants and excess nutrients and restoring ground water reserves. Credit: Laura Miller RLA

A serene seating area also serves to absorb runoff with its water loving plantings. A rain garden can be designed to complement any style of garden.

A planting of native wildflowers absorbs runoff from a museum parking lot. Plantings such as this can help to prevent stream pollution and flooding. Credit: Laura Miller, RLA

There are numerous possibilities for restoring natural water systems such as the wetland associated with this golf course. Credit: Land-Studies Inc.

Chapter 1
Sustaining Life on Earth

"Children of a culture born in a water-rich environment, we have never really learned how important water is to us. We understand it, but we do not respect it."
William Ashworth, *Nor Any Drop to Drink*, 1982

A cool refreshing glass of water, a hot shower, cooking and cleaning, swimming and boating, food production, maintaining our gardens, ponds and fountains, serene water views…we take water for granted because our supply of clean water is plentiful in the United States. However, interest in conservation is growing rapidly as more and more people become concerned with water quality and quantity for today and tomorrow. Whether you are thinking about your impact on global environmental issues or are troubled by a soil wash-out, a damp basement, or a soggy lawn in your home landscape, there are ways you can help with the problem. At the community and regional level these solutions can be applied on a larger scale.

For centuries mankind has taken from the earth all that we needed, with little concern about exhausting supplies and disturbing natural processes. In the past whole civilizations have died out as a result of resource depletion. (See Jared Diamon's *Collapse: How Societies Choose to Fail or Succeed*; Viking Penguin, 2005). Today burgeoning populations are resulting in an alarming rate of over consumption of many resources. One of the most critical threats to human existence is a shortage of *clean* water. Along with water shortages, there are other environmental impacts related to water management. A few of them are flooding, erosion, and impacts on food supplies. In some regions, land subsidence or "sink holes" have appeared as underground reservoirs are drained empty and collapse. Salt water may infiltrate aquifers as fresh water is pumped out, further reducing the drinking water supply, fresh water fisheries, and agricultural crops.

As earth scientists have issued dire warnings about dwindling water quality and supplies, many communities have begun to search for ways of conserving this valuable resource. Observation of undisturbed natural areas has revealed the hydrologic cycle, a very effective system for preserving and cleaning water while controlling flooding. Environmental

Rain gardens help to protect our streams and waterways for recreational use and food production by cleansing water and allowing it to trickle slowly instead of gush into waterways. Restoring natural processes modifies drought/flood cycles. Credit: LandStudies Inc.

planners are studying ways of restoring the hydrologic cycle so that storm water runoff is purified and re-circulated, while impact on waterways is reduced. Wise community planners and homeowners are striving to restore natural processes in an attempt to develop more balanced and ecologically sound management of water resources. A few positive developments are advanced paving materials that allow water to infiltrate the soil; protection and restoration of wetlands and estuaries; reforestation; low impact development, and bio-retention basins, or as they are popularly known, rain gardens.

The hydrologic cycle is a basic support system for life on earth. How does it work? In its natural state, much of the land is covered in dense vegetation. Trees, with an understory of plants and shrubs, carpet forested regions and dense, deep-rooted, prairie grasses cover the plains. This vegetative growth constantly rebuilds soil as it maintains moisture at healthy levels. In both forest and prairie, deep, spreading, roots provide a structure for holding soil in place against wind and water erosion responsible for the degradation of arable land and the silting of streams and rivers. We disrupt this cycle at our own risk.

Headlines tell of more frequent and severe flooding with extensive damage, loss of property and life. Much of this catastrophic flooding is the result of faulty land management practices such as flood plain destruction and overdevelopment. When vegetation has been stripped away and the earth is covered with paving and roofs, storm water rushes off these impervious surfaces and through piped drainage systems, into surface waterways such as ditches, small streams, and rivers. Water, rushing through those waterways, at great velocity, cuts deeply into the earth. These deep channels further constrict the flow of water and result in an increase in the destructive force of storm water. At the same time, excessive nutrients, waste products, and chemicals known as non-point pollution, are washed along with surface water into our bays, estuaries, and oceans. This non-point pollution jeopardizes valuable fisheries and recreational resources. We only have to look around us or read the headlines to see the results of disruption of the hydrologic cycle due to poor land and water management.

Petroleum products and other pollutants wash off parking lots. This rain garden holds pollutants in soil and mulch layers as it restores ground water reserves. Credit: Laura Miller RLA

An illustration of Hydrologic Cycle showing the cycle of evapo-transpiration and precipitation on which all life depends. Precipitation falls from the clouds. Some of it is preserved as snow. As snow melts and rain falls runoff is slowed by vegetation and held so that it seeps into the soil to support plant life. Some of it seeps further into bedrock aquifers and some of it flows into small streams. Streams empty into rivers, lakes, and bays and eventually into the oceans.

As rain falls on forests and plains, leaves and stalks, layers of plant litter and matted roots capture water and slowly release it to soak into the soil. Roots serve several purposes in the water cycle. They absorb water to carry nutrients through plant systems. Deep roots also create a channel for surface water to follow as it makes its way down toward underground reservoirs or aquifers. Roots also hold soil in place and prevent erosion. Some prairie grass roots penetrate more than six feet into the soil. Plants take up moisture and minerals through their roots, and give off water vapor through their leaves in a process called transpiration. This process cools the surrounding air and returns moisture to the atmosphere to collect in clouds.

In heavy rainfall or snow-melt, runoff trickles downward. This water is slowed and filtered through the plant growth, roots, and surface litter. Clean, clear water flows gently into streams, rivers, and bays where it is stored until it evaporates and returns to the atmosphere. Clouds gather from water vapor given off by plants through evapo-transpiration from waterways and soil. When atmospheric conditions dictate, water returns to the earth as rain, snow, sleet, fog, or hale. That is a very simplified explanation of the Hydrologic Cycle that supports all life on earth. Desertification, the conversion of fertile land to desert, is the result of interrupting this cycle by removing one or more of its components.

Housing and urban development is one way we interrupt the hydrologic cycle. When the builder begins work, vegetation is stripped from the soil. As it rains, a torrent of water rushes over the unprotected earth, eroding soil and picking up pollutants. The ecological balance of waterways is disrupted when this muddy water cascades into nearby streams. These muddied and polluted waters empty into larger waterways—rivers, lakes, and estuaries—eventually reaching the oceans. Both fresh water and ocean fisheries are threatened and aquatic life cycles are

An early morning photograph captures water vapor being released into the atmosphere from the landscape. This is an example of evapo-transpiration.

A community rain garden near Ephrata, Pennsylvania, creates a scenic recreation area while protecting the adjacent stream from pollution and flooding. Credit: LandStudies Inc.

disrupted. Drinking water resources are polluted. Soil structure and fertility are destroyed.

As development proceeds, vegetation is replaced by roofs, pavement, and lawns. These surfaces act much like bare soil, allowing water to gush over them, picking up excess nutrients, chemical residues, heavy metals, and other pollutants. Lawn grasses are supported by frequently-applied chemical insecticides and fertilizers. At the same time lawns, unlike meadows, forests, and planting beds, allow runoff at a rate very similar to paved surfaces. Paved surfaces collect petroleum residues and toxic substances used in the construction process and in our day-to-day activities. The EPA claims that storm water runoff from urban areas is the leading pollutant of rivers and lakes. As this high volume of runoff dumps directly into waterways, even with modest rainfall, small streams and rivers become torrents and overflow their banks.

You can see how development contributes to flooding and depletion of water resources before anyone turns on a tap. In response to flooding and pollution, engineers and scientists have attempted to mitigate the situation. With currently accepted technology we build levees, pipe streams underground, and treat our drinking water with harsh chemicals. As an outcome of these measures we are faced with the degradation of commercially valuable fish stocks and unsightly polluted and dying waterways. We have already lost the recreational value of many lakes and rivers. Flooding is an ever-growing problem as more and more land is covered with waterproof surfaces such as roofs and roadways. People turn to expensive bottled water for drinking, to avoid the chemicals used to purify municipal water supplies. The plastic waste generated by discarded water bottles adds to our environmental problems.

Where Does Rain Go?

When rain falls on land covered by natural dense vegetation 10 percent of the water acts as runoff, 50 percent infiltrates into soil to restore ground water and maintain plant life, and 40 percent is given off as water vapor by transpiration and evaporation.

A suburban development results in 30 percent runoff, 25 percent infiltration, and 35 percent evaporation/transpiration.

A city results in 55 percent runoff, 15 percent infiltration, and 30 percent evaporation/transpiration.

A restored wetland fulfills the function of a naturally occurring wetland. The lively greens and flowers are part of the charm. Wildlife is drawn to the water and habitat of this planting. Credit: LandStudies Inc.

Small residential rain gardens collect water from a garage roof and driveway as they create a pleasing view from the house. Credit: Terry Wallace

As the climate changes, the occurrence of both extended drought and torrential rain, are ever more common occurrences. Although we humans like to think that we have control over our environment, recent climate events have shown us very clearly that we are at the mercy of natural forces. We must learn to adapt to and work with these environmental forces if we are to enjoy a comfortable standard of living. As this book is being written severe drought is threatening Georgia while floods are raging in Texas, Kansas, and Missouri. The rescue, clean up, and support of flood survivors will cost state and local governments billions of dollars. The cost to private business, insurance companies, and industries within the flood zone will be more billions. In addition there is the economic impact of lost jobs from businesses that are driven to bankruptcy by flood damage. All of these losses however, are minor when measured against the loss of life and the suffering of families who lose all that they have worked for as a result of floods. We cannot afford to ignore this problem.

Past efforts at environmental control have often resulted in unintended consequences, some far worse than the elements we attempt to control. One example is levee systems designed to prevent flooding of riverside towns and low-lying areas. The result has often been inundation of upstream or downstream populations or truly catastrophic floods when levees fail in the force of a storm. Levees give a false sense of security and lead to massive destruction and loss of life when they can't stand up to the forces of nature. We saw this unfortunate impact when Hurricanes Katrina and Rita struck New Orleans.

With careful community planning, land and water management, expensive and unattractive levees would be unnecessary. Another example of misguided efforts to control water runoff is currently accepted storm water drainage systems. Rainwater and snow melt from our streets and neighborhoods is collected and piped directly into rivers, bays, and even estuaries. Ground water reserves are bypassed and depleted. Water gushes into waterways at a much greater volume than is natural. Surface pollutants from roadways, roofs, and lawns are carried with the storm water. The result is disrupted ecosystems, pollution, and flooding.

In heavy storms and floods, surface water finds its way into sewage treatment and drinking water systems. There it has a negative impact on the processes used to cleanse water. It often overwhelms water-handling capacity, resulting in sewage spills, which contribute to unsafe drinking water and serious pollution of streams and rivers, destruction of fresh-water fish stocks, and adds recreation potential. All this contributes to the looming specter of running out of fresh water supplies as a result of environmental degradation.

It's not all gloom and doom however. As scientists study nature's water management systems they are finding ways to use those processes to reduce the impact of storm water and drought on our communities. Among them, the bio-retention basin or rain garden is a method many landowners are adopting. It is a simple method of using natural processes for cleansing water and replenishing supplies. Instead of being piped away, water is collected and filtered through soil into underground reservoirs called aquifers. A rain garden helps to stabilize the hydrologic cycle of evaporation, condensation, and precipitation, which replenishes surface water and supports plant and animal life on earth. At the same time impurities, including fertilizers, pesticides, chemicals, and heavy metals, known as non-point pollution, are filtered out. The benefits of protecting water resources are many.

Intelligent water resource management improves the environment by:

• Increasing the amount of clean water in natural reservoirs.

• Filtering out non-point pollution carried by storm water runoff.

• Reducing soil erosion, drought and flooding.

• Restoring the hydrologic cycle

Surface water puddles on this wet lawn. Excessive moisture and poor drainage has killed most of the plantings and contributed to the decay of the fence.

The same scene with a rain garden surrounding a small pond. The garden is designed to collect excess water from the surrounding lawn, roof, and sump pump. These plants will thrive in the moist environment and yet they will withstand periods of dryness when the clay soil is baked hard. A mulch layer helps to filter nutrients and pollutants before they reach the pond.

Undulating beds of daylilies collect runoff from roof, terraces and lawns. Rain gardens do not require native plants or an untamed appearance. Credit: Richard Lyon RLA

A tribute to rain by Belgium sculptor and artist Jean-Michel Folon.

A rain garden doubles as a wildlife refuge. A heated water station is hidden from view just behind the shrubbery. Adirondack chairs add color and provide seating for enjoyment of the changing scene.

Chapter 2
What is a Rain Garden?

"Man – despite his artistic pretensions, his sophistication, and his many accomplishments – owes his existence to a six-inch layer of topsoil and the fact that it rains."

Unknown author

Bioswale Section View

LandStudies

A cross section of a bio-swale or rain garden. This sketch shows how a bio-swale restores the hydrologic cycle. Credit: LandStudies Inc.

A rain garden is a system for restoring some of the function that is lost when land is developed. It is simply a shallow basin with a porous backfill and deep rooted, moisture tolerant plantings. It is located where it will collect runoff from downspouts, sump pumps, paved areas, roofs and expanses of lawn. It can be one large garden or a number of smaller depressions within a larger garden or border. It takes about three years from planting to becoming a fully functioning, low maintenance rain garden. Notice I said low maintenance, not no maintenance. All gardens require some degree of effort to remain attractive and healthy.

Early rain gardens were designed primarily for function with less thought given to their long-term appearance and maintenance requirements. Many of these gardens were based on the prairie model. The focus was on using native species and grasses. Some of those early rain gardens were abandoned because suburban homeowners did not enjoy the "wild" appearance of the native plant populations or they found maintenance to be burdensome. With expanded interest and demand, many landscape architects have become interested in designing aesthetically pleasing and sustainable schemes. While native riparian species are still widely used, it is also possible to create rain gardens with common, moisture tolerant, garden plants. A few examples are Astilbe, Hosta, Daylilies, and Siberian Iris. (See Chapter 5: Rain Garden Plants)

Water loving grasses and cannas soak up storm water from nearby roofs and pavements.

Rain Gardens through the Seasons

A rain garden can be designed for a formal appearance or a more casual look, depending upon the surrounding landscape and the aesthetic values of the homeowner. Today many firms specialize in ecological based landscape design, including rain gardens. When searching for a design firm to work with, you must be very clear about your objectives, with particular emphasis on the appearance you desire.

A drainage swale may already be designed into your landscape. Frequently these swales become filled with silt from runoff, which in effect changes the grade so that they no longer keep water moving away from the structure. Instead of draining, such a swale may actually hold water and become a marsh during winter and spring. With re-grading such a swale can be diverted into a rain garden, which will handle the excess runoff. While it may not always dry up a damp basement, it certainly makes sense to direct the downspouts and other runoff away from the house foundation and into the rain garden.

A grouping of native plants as they occur naturally. There is a popular movement today to use natural appearing grouping of plants to create low maintenance gardens. This style does not suit every style of landscape or every taste.

One way to contribute to improved municipal water management is to remove downspouts from public storm sewer systems and channel them into a rain garden or rain collection system. (See Chapter 9: Everyday Water Conservation.)

As much as twelve gallons of rainwater per minute can gush from a downspout during a rainstorm. Removing that pressure from storm water systems will greatly improve water management efforts in your community. Of course the rain garden must be designed to handle the increased volume of water it receives. Future chapters will include ideas and formulas for a homeowner to use in determining the size and depth needed. However, in the case of steeply sloping land or an excessive amount of water flowing into the property from surrounding terrain, an expert should be consulted. Some state and local government agencies, municipalities, and private organizations will provide assistance.

Spring. Grasses in a wet mesic meadow are slow to develop in the cool weather of spring. As the season grows warmer they quickly fill out the meadow. Wildflowers add color and attract beneficial insects, birds, and butterflies.

Summer. A collection of summer blooming plants suitable for a rain garden includes Joe Pye Weed, Brown-eyed Susan, and Sneeze-weed. This exuberant planting requires very low maintenance.

A rain garden can be a family project. Children enjoy seeing the results of their labor as the garden develops. They also enjoy wildlife as it moves into a newly created habitat. Credit: LandStudies Inc.

The functional purpose of a rain garden is to collect runoff, hold water and filter it as it percolates into ground-water. Many pollutants are broken down through com-posting processes that take place in organic mulches and soil. Insoluble pollutants such as heavy metals will be absorbed and held in mulch layers. While those are the main functions of a rain garden, there are several secondary benefits. Many of us gain pleasure from observing seasonal changes. In a well-designed rain garden, there are spring flow-ers, cool green vegetation, autumn foliage color, berries, and graceful grasses to be enjoyed throughout the year.

Developing and maintaining a rain garden is a family project that will be remembered for a lifetime. It offers an opportunity to teach children the importance of protecting our environment while allowing them to participate in conservation by planting and maintaining the garden. It may attract valuable wildlife, such as birds, butterflies and amphibians, which are often driven to extinction in our communities by habitat destruction. Children who are comfortable with and enjoy observing wildlife will grow up realizing the value of protecting fragile habitats against encroachment and destruction.

Fall. A rain garden border in autumn. Water from the roof and terrace are collected in this four-season border.

Winter. Inkberry, Red Twig Dogwood, and Dried grass stalks lend lively color and texture to the same border.

Maintaining a wildlife habitat is great way to involve children and help reinforce good environmental practices. The National Wildlife Federation recognizes those who provide a backyard wildlife habitat. When you have met the criteria for a certified wildlife habitat and sent the application fee, you will receive a personalized certificate. NWF also maintains a national registry of certified habitats. Once certified you may purchase an attractive sign to identify your Wildlife Habitat. To qualify for certification the habitat must include the following:

• Food Sources: Native plants, seeds, fruits, nuts, berries, nectar

• Water Sources: A birdbath, pond, stream

• Places for cover: Thicket, rockpile, or birdhouse

• Places to raise young: Dense shrubs or trees, nesting boxes, pond

• Sustainable Gardening practices such as mulch, compost, rain garden, chemical free gardening practices.

• For more information or to apply go to www.nwf.org/backyard/certify.cfm.

This rain garden has been abandoned by the homeowners. Although it is unattractive in appearance, it is still functioning to collect storm water and filter it into ground water reserves.

Top left:
A very different
type of garden
is this woodland
path. It too works
to soak up run-
off and restore
groundwater.

Bottom left:
A small planting of
moisture tolerant
plants keeps paths
from washing out
and puddling after
storms.

A small pond enhances the charm of a rain garden and acts as a wildlife magnet.

    To avoid mosquito breeding, water should not stand on the surface of a rain garden for more than four days. If the rain garden does not drain within that time it becomes a wetland, bog garden, or a pond, depending upon the depth of standing water. Each of these can be maintained as an environmentally healthy garden feature, but they are technically not rain gardens and they will require extra effort to remain healthy and serve the purpose of a rain garden. Some rain gardens may have a pond or bog associated with them.

    If a pond is to be part of your rain garden it will need a system to clean and aerate water. The rain garden itself can be used to cleanse the pond by re-circulating water through the established plants and allowing it to seep back into the pond. This can be a fairly simple system, but installation directions are beyond the scope of this book. Please consult a pond management expert if you are planning to combine your rain garden with a pond feature. For additional ideas and information, please refer to *Natural Swimming Pools: Inspiration for Harmony with Nature* by Michael Littlewood.

Chapter 3

Community Efforts or "Beautiful Solutions to Water Pollution"

"Water is life's matter and matrix, mother and medium. There is no life without water."

Albert Szent-Gyorgyi,
Hungarian biochemist and Nobel Prize Winner for Medicine

*O*ne municipality took the lead in experimenting with storm water management. Prince Georges County, Maryland, was a pioneer in adopting systems to collect water from paved and roofed areas such as shopping centers, housing developments, and municipal buildings. Bio-retention basins were designed and installed by county personnel to test their effectiveness in handling runoff. Much was learned from these early efforts in the mid 1980s. Rain garden islands provided significant aesthetic enhancement of parking lots surrounding shopping centers and large housing tracts while absorbing and filtering storm water.

Puddling and erosion problems were greatly reduced or eliminated while petroleum laden scum that washed off parking lots could be observed covering gravel mulches at inlets to the gardens. The environmental benefits were so positive that in addition to creating municipal rain gardens, Prince Georges County and the State of Maryland now make resources and guidelines available to encourage homeowners to build their own rain gardens.

Around the country many communities have been influ-

A wetland is being created to offset another destroyed during development. Credit: Laura Miller RLA

enced by Prince Georges County's pioneering efforts. Today numerous websites offer guidelines for those attempting to construct their own bio-retention basins. The Wisconsin Department of Natural Resources has a comprehensive website offering a how-to-manual, plant lists, articles, and photos of rain gardens around the state. Part of the website is devoted to volunteer groups under the umbrella of Water Action Volunteers, which provides educational programs, materials, and support for water resource monitoring and conservation projects through the work of local organizations such as 4H, student groups, and citizen volunteers.

This serene and tranquil scene is a healthy wetland after restoration. A wetland can be aesthetically pleasing while it supports the hydrologic cycle. Credit: Laura Miller RLA

A rain garden island softens an expanse of pavement while it collects storm water. Credit: Laura Miller RLA

Petroleum laden scum coats these river stones as it washes off a parking lot. The rain garden removes many surface pollutants from water as it percolates through plants, mulch, and soil. Credit: Laura Miller RLA.

A roadside burger stop contributes to a better environment by maintaining a rain garden in the parking area. Credit: Laura Miller RLA

A rain garden absorbs runoff from an expansive roof and parking lot surrounding a municipal maintenance building. Credit: LandStudies Inc.

A restored flood plain allows storm water to rise and fall without destructive force. This meandering path is the normal pattern of small streams. When such channels are filled in, straightened, piped, or otherwise modified, storm water may reach such great velocity that it destroys everything in its path. Credit: LandStudies Inc.

Lititz, a rural community in Pennsylvania, has taken progressive action to protect water resources and reduce small stream flooding. Land Studies, a firm of landscape architects led by Mark and Kelly Gutshall, have found answers to many of the challenges of small stream flood control and storm water management. By studying the natural waterways of Southeastern Pennsylvania, they have developed steps to restore the water conservation and flood control capability of natural stream systems. In the restored floodplain systems, high velocity currents with the capacity to do great damage can become low-energy sheet flows, which subside harmlessly as they return water to aquifers and established stream channels. The large bio-retention basins created to achieve this purpose have become beautiful natural areas where locals enjoy the changing seasons and the restoration of wildlife habitat.

Rain Gardens of West Michigan, a 501C3 organization was founded as a cooperative effort of private citizens, businesses and the City of Grand Rapids, Michigan. The organization has grown far beyond the original vision of founder Patricia Pennell who was inspired by the Prince George's County rain garden movement. Their tag line which emphasizes the great economic, social, and environmental benefits of the movement is "Saving the Great Lakes, One Rain Garden at a Time". Their effort to achieve, "Beautiful solutions to water pollution", has inspired a rapidly growing movement among citizens of Western Michigan.

The State of Virginia, Department of Forestry website is an excellent resource for technical information for homeowners wishing to create a rain garden. The information is presented in a clear easily followed format. In addition they offer links to several technical publications on the subject. Most states have at least one website dedicated to water management.

The independent organization 10,000 Rain Gardens maintains a comprehensive website with a wealth of information on water resource conservation and protection. Another environmental organization, Rain Garden Network, located in Chicago, was formed to offer citizens solutions to non-point pollution problems throughout the country. In cooperation with Ecotone Media and Citizen Solution, they sponsor electronic and print media, on site assistance, education and outreach programs.

There are numerous additional resources on the internet and through local and state governments and private organizations. I mention a few of the most comprehensive and I am encouraged by a growing interest and demand for information about water resource conservation. The fact that you have picked up this book and are reading it is yet another reason for optimism in the effort to better manage water resources. Check with your local department of natural resources or environmental protection. Some municipalities, such as the City of Milwaukee, offer grant money to help defray the cost of installing a rain garden. Many more offer technical information and assistance for planning the installation. I have included a list of informative websites sponsored by public and private organizations in the glossary. However a search of the internet will likely turn up many new sites that did not exist at this writing.

A restored wetland creates a community recreation area and wildlife habitat. Credit: LandStudies Inc.

A newly planted rain garden will collect runoff from a large parking lot adjacent to it. The stone mulch helps to stabilize soil, preventing silting and washouts. Credit: Laura Miller RLA.

Hockessin Green
A Successful Community Rain Garden

Housing development in New Castle County, Delaware, has exploded in the last twenty years. Where fields and forests once covered the land, the suburb of Hockessin has seen explosive growth of new neighborhoods as nearby Wilmington became a thriving economic center. As each new development was planned, a traditional storm water detention basin was part of the design. More often than not, no mention of maintaining these basins was made to new homebuyers.

Years later these storm water systems started to fail, resulting in flooding and the creation of health hazards. In the year 2000, of the 454 neighborhoods in New Castle County, 75 had clogged and failing drainage systems. The county moved in and issued summons to residents. The failing systems had to be fixed and Hockessin Green was one of those neighborhoods.

After costly failed attempts to correct the problem themselves, community leaders turned to their local government for guidance and help in improving surface water management. They found those resources available in the form of State of Delaware funding and technical assistance. Community residents welcomed the new information on the best ways to establish a system that handles storm water effectively while resisting invasive species and insect problems. With a new plan in place they went to work on the problem once more. After installation they joined in to maintain the bio-retention basin in the early years. The outcome of this community action is an attractive and sustainable storm water management area.

Many, if not most, neighborhoods will eventually face storm water management problems. Carefully designed and maintained private and community rain gardens are an attractive and affordable solution. In New Castle County, Delaware, workshops are conducted several times a year by White Clay Creek Wild and Scenic River Association in cooperation with the National Park Service and the Delaware Coastal Program. Check with your state to find local resources for storm water management practices. (From an article by Andrea Miller in *The Community News*, February 16, 2007)

This tranquil path leads through the Sustainable Rain Garden, one of several gardens in the arboretum at Temple University's Ambler Campus. The arboretum allows landscape architecture students to experience firsthand the impact of gardening practices on the environment. The gardens are open to the public.

Many colleges and universities are implementing and studying rain gardens as a way of managing their own storm water and as an example for homeowner and communities. Temple University has created successful bio-retention basins to manage storm water runoff at their Ambler Pennsylvania campus. One of several example and teaching gardens at that campus, the Sustainable Wetland Garden was established in 1998. Many principles of sustainable design are demonstrated by this garden. Some of them are: the use of recycled materials for all construction, the use of solar energy to power a pump that recirculates water through the fountain, collection of rainwater from roofs and biological filtration of runoff.

The garden replaces a grassy swale that was designed to carry storm water away from buildings. Instead it became a boggy mess, difficult to mow and unattractive. The new garden evolved as succeeding landscape architecture classes studied and learned from it. Some plantings were deemed too invasive and removed while a slightly modified planting scheme contributed to a more attractive appearance. Special emphasis has been placed on the sensory experiences of fragrance, color, shifting light and shadow and the sounds of running water, rustling vegetation and bird song.

Local stone and gravel were used to harmonize with the native plantings. No pesticides, herbicides or artificial fertilizers are used to maintain this plot. This garden has been so successful that another rain garden is under development to manage runoff from the roof and pavement of a new campus building. Temple's Ambler PA campus is a worthwhile destination for those interested in gardens of all types and rain gardens in particular.

A sun powered fountain in the Ambler Campus rain garden. Most materials used to create the garden are recycled including mulch and construction materials.

A community rain garden has become a favorite spot for family outings and picnicking. Credit: LandStudies Inc.

Chapter 4

Planning and Designing Your Rain Garden

"Water is the lifeblood of our bodies, our economy, our nation and our well-being."

Stephen Johnson, EPA Administrator, El Paso, TX, 2007

A rain garden is a beautiful way of using nature's own bio-filtration system for preserving and cleansing ground water. It is a garden to be enjoyed throughout the seasons while it does serious work. A rain garden can be adapted in size, style, color, and texture to suit any taste and to complement any style of home architecture. For those who enjoy observing wildlife, it can become a magnet and refuge for birds, butterflies, and beneficial amphibians. These benefits are bonuses, in addition to the main purpose of a rain garden, which is to soak up urban and suburban runoff, filter out impurities, and reduce incidents of flooding by recreating nature's own water management system. Also known as a bio-retention basin, a rain garden acts much like a natural system to collect surface water, purify it, and return clean water to the earth making it available for drinking and other uses. As water is collected in the rain garden, it slowly percolates through layers of mulch and soil, pollutants are removed and held in the material or absorbed by plants.

Rain Gardens need not be large and elaborate to help control runoff. These small pockets collect storm water from moderate sized properties, retain and recycle it. Credit: Laura Miller RLA

A homeowner who is willing to do some study and research may be able to design and implement an attractive rain garden for an average property with minor runoff issues. There is a wealth of information available, on the internet as indicated in previous chapters and in this publication. Do not rush the design process. It takes time to work through the functional and aesthetic issues involved and time spent in planning may prevent regrets later on.

When planning a rain garden or any excavation, the first two considerations must be identifying municipal permitting requirements and locating existing utilities and property boundaries. Municipal codes can be found at county or township buildings or websites. The county or township engineers office is a good place to start asking. Most water, gas, cable, phone, and electric utilities can be flagged for you by a local agency set up by the utility companies for this purpose. If you are not sure who to call, check your local electricity supplier's website. You will be excavating from six to twenty-four inches for the rain garden, so it is very important to have those utilities marked and to avoid positioning the rain garden immediately over them or striking them while digging. In immediate danger of damage are electric dog fences, which may be just a few inches beneath the soil surface and which the local utility supplier will not flag.

If the runoff volume is very large or the slope exceeds 12 percent, it is best to consult an experienced design professional. A landscape architect, civil engineer, or hydrologist will survey the area that drains into the rain garden. Then he or she will evaluate the soil type and structure to determine its absorption and percolation capacity. To do this several tests may be performed such as a core sample and a percolation test. With this information, he or she can calculate how large the rain garden needs to be and where it should be located to handle the estimated quantity of runoff. Be sure to consult a professional designer who has training and experience in surface water management if you have serious runoff and erosion problems or difficult terrain.

Not every landscape designer or architect is trained and experienced in this type of design. Take time to search out a firm that specializes in the field of water management. Ask to see some projects and talk with past clients. There are few issues that can cause more damage and anxiety to a homeowner than uncontrolled water problems, so be sure your investment is applied effectively in managing storm water.

If you decide to design a rain garden yourself, the next step is to determine the size and location. Future chapters contain guidelines for determining the area needed to handle runoff. Before you begin to design, determine the approximate square footage of rain garden you will need to for water management. Outline the approximate square footage using hoses or stakes and twine. Seeing the space required will help you visualize the finished garden as you begin to plan.

A rain garden with lawn strip buffer collects water from roof and parking areas, protecting a nearby creek from overload and pollution during storms. Even though this parking lot is paved with loose aggregate there is some runoff. The lawn serves as a pre-filtration system, removing some particulate and chemical pollution. Credit: Laura Miller RLA

An exuberant collection of native plants in the rain garden at Temple University's Ambler Campus. Smaller plants and groundcovers edging the path give it the garden a groomed appearance. Shredded materials from campus landscape maintenance activities are recycled as mulch in this garden.

The bold textures of a naturally occurring meadow is the model for a new garden design trend often referred to as *Natural Gardens, Woodland Gardens*, or even *Bold, Romantic Gardens* wherein plants are arranged in much the way that they would occur naturally. This style reduces maintenance and presents a wide range of seasonal changes.

Think of the rain garden as an integral part of your landscape instead of an add-on. For the best effect design the rain garden like any other bed by applying the elements of good design. (For general landscape design information see my book *Landscaping for the Mid-Atlantic*, published by Schiffer Publishing). A rain garden should always blend with the larger planting scheme. One or more small rain gardens can be seamlessly incorporated into a large bed or border. Water always runs downhill so it is obvious that the rain garden needs to be downhill from the sources of runoff. The lowest point of the property is often a good place to start; However, there may be intermediate collection points, particularly if there is a history of torrential rainfalls and excessive runoff. If your garden is formal, precise and sculpted, the rain garden should have a similar appearance. Most rain gardens are designed in an informal style, but don't hesitate to design a symmetrical and carefully controlled garden if it fits your landscape style and preference. In such a formal setting, choose plants with a trim, orderly appearance. Some plants such as Maiden Grass and arborvitae are very neat and uniform in appearance and can be used in a formal design with little more than a spring trimming.

A simple planting of Fern, Hydrangea, and American Dogwood create a lovely small shade garden. The dogwood would not be suitable for a driveway or parking lot rain garden since it does not tolerate salt and pollution runoff. The native Dogwood will tolerate intermittent high moisture levels.

For a casual look you could combine native and common garden plants in a cottage garden style. For those who enjoy the look of a natural environment, there is a wealth of plants and examples to draw from. In this style the objective is to combine native plants in much the same way that they occur naturally.

Whether you choose native or common garden plants, pay attention to size. Very tall grasses and perennials will look their best near the center of a bed or the back of a border with intermediate and short plants nearer the edges. Some native plants may have an "out of control" appearance as the summer progresses. An edging of low growing, easily maintained plantings surrounding the rain garden will keep it looking neat and attractive throughout the season. Be sure to include plants with berries and some evergreen material to keep the garden interesting throughout the winter months.

Carefree Viburnum, Hosta, and Asters combine to create a low maintenance rain garden that is attractive throughout the growing season.

If you have a septic tank and drain field, do not locate a rain garden directly over them. The extra water may unbalance those systems and cause them to fail. It is equally important to determine your property boundaries to avoid encroachment on a neighboring property. Just as you would not plant trees or place a fence on your neighbor's property, the rain garden needs to be contained within your own boundaries. It is not acceptable to direct runoff onto a neighboring property. Sometimes neighbors will go together and develop a common rain garden. This can be risky because neighbors may move and the new owners may not share your interest. It is very important to understand your municipality's right-of-way restraints and water management codes. In many municipalities a permit is required for any soil disturbance. Check on your local ordinances before you design or dig.

Finally, since water collected in a rain garden will percolate back into the soil, it should be placed some distance from buildings. The rule of thumb for placement is that a rain garden should be no less than ten feet from a foundation. That rule can be modified somewhat depending on grades and property size. If you have already identified a low area in your lawn, it is relatively easy to place the rain garden where water collects naturally. However, if surface water stands in that area for long periods, it is not an appropriate site since the rain garden needs to allow runoff to percolate quickly into the subsoil.

Native and cultivated plants combine to create a colorful scene.

Measure the property and sketch it at a workable scale, indicating the location of structures, trees, utilities, and septic tank/drain field, if applicable. This is your plot plan. Now collect a few pencils and a roll or pad of tracing paper. With your best determination of the size of basin you need and the approximate location, start playing with shapes. Place the tracing paper over your plot plan and work out the shape that best suits your taste. The garden can extend beyond the retention basin if needed to create a pleasing outline. A very large rain garden is often divided into two or more smaller areas for ease of installation and maintenance.

To catch most of the runoff, the long side of your garden should run across the slope and the short side should go up and down the slope. On a steeper hill the garden may be sized smaller and deeper to manage the same amount of runoff. Try to avoid the drip line of large trees to prevent damage to the tree as well as difficulty in excavation. If possible locate the rain garden where it can be seen from the house so you can enjoy the results of your hard work.

Browse through the photos in this book for garden shapes and plant combinations you find pleasing. Many websites listed in the glossary also contain photos of rain gardens of various styles and stages of development. There is no need to start from scratch. If you see a pleasing garden design, adapt it to your needs. As you live with your garden it will evolve to reflect your own taste, even if you start with an example from a book or website. Most gardeners make adjustments to plantings over time, as new ideas occur to them or some plants don't perform as expected. Occasionally a combination of plants doesn't look as pleasing as you thought it would. Expect to make adjustments and additions for the first few growing seasons. Annuals can be added in the early years to fill in empty space and for seasonal color if you choose. The level of maintenance gardening required for your rain garden is largely a matter of design, from occasional maintenance to more or less continual puttering.

When you have designated a tentative area and shape for the rain garden, mark it out with lime, temporary paint, or string and stakes. Walk around and observe it from all sides. Visualize how this new garden will fit in with your existing or planned landscape. To evaluate placement of trees, a long pole or even a shovel driven into the ground will help you to conceptualize vertical elements. Overturned baskets or large pots may be useful in estimating the effect of shrubs and perennials. Many of us have difficulty envisioning the end result from a plan on paper or a simple outline on the ground. If you have a friend with an artistic eye you might want to ask for his or her opinion of your garden's form. In the end, you are the one who will look out at your garden every day, so be sure it is pleasing to your eye.

Since the rain garden will form a shallow basin, soil will be excavated and amended and some of it will not be returned to the rain garden. Excess soil is used as a berm or embankment to retain water on the downhill end of the rain garden. Berms should be gently rounded and tapered much like naturally rolling landforms. The berm at the low end of a rain garden should be equal in elevation to the uphill edge. Plan on planting and mulching this berm to prevent erosion and to retain its shape. The soil berm will drain and dry quickly, so choose plantings accordingly. Wetland plants may not thrive in the berms well-drained soil. Excess soil can also be spread over low areas of poor drainage to raise the grade and encourage water to flow toward the rain garden.

When designing, provide for channels for runoff to follow into the rain garden. Downspouts and sump pumps can be directed into a 4-inch plastic pipe that is buried beneath the soil and empties into the rain garden. Surface water can be channeled with shallow swales. Steeper swales may be lined with landscape fabric and one to three inch or larger river washed stone. Broad, shallow, swales may be sodded. Sod should be secured with pins to hold it in place until roots develop.

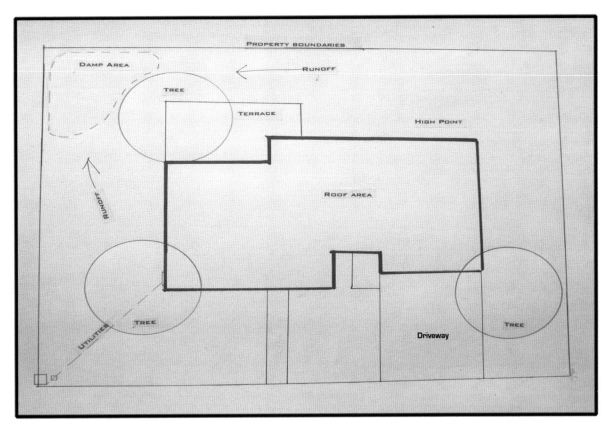

Plot Plan drawn to scale

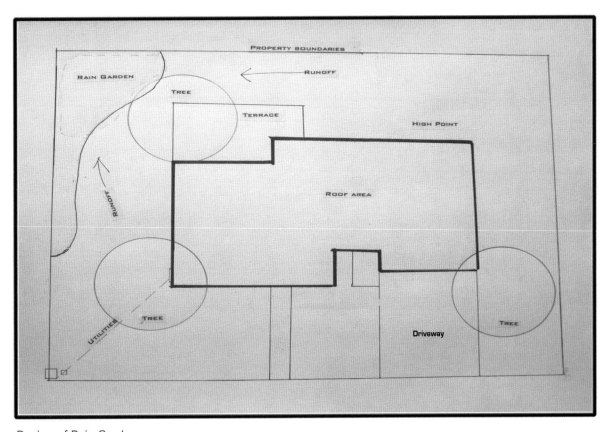

Design of Rain Garden

A rain garden border can be attractive in every season. Here Redtwig Dogwood, Maiden Grass and Inkberry Holly shine against the snow.

Seven Steps to Creating Your Rain Garden

1. Check with municipal authorities for permitting requirements. Determine property boundaries, locations of septic system and all underground utilities
2. Measure the area that will drain into the rain garden. Test soil percolation capacity. Determine degree of slope on land. Determine size of rain garden needed.
3. Design rain garden. Select plants.
4. Mark out bed and excavate to the depth indicated.
5. Amend soil with compost and coarse sand as indicated by soil type. Refill bed to within 6 inches of surrounding grade. Use remaining soil to create berm on downhill side of bed.
6. Plant and mulch.
7. Water, add birdbath and birdhouses, sculpture, and fountain as you desire. Add seating nearby and enjoy watching your rain garden go to work.

The best plan, if you have room, is to grade for sheet drainage. That is a broad, shallow, slope that allows water to spread over a large area as it makes it way into the rain garden. A healthy lawn will be adequate to secure the soil over this area. When water sheets it loses much of its velocity and therefore is not as likely to carry soil away.

Chapter five contains lists of trees, shrubbery, and perennials that tolerate flooding and some standing water. These same plants will tolerate hard baked soil during dry months. If you try to use every plant on the list, your rain garden will end up looking like a jungle. Consider a few plants that are well suited to the landscape style, soil type, light level and climate of your garden and use them in masses or sweeps. Repetition of major elements, such as trees, and shrubbery will result in a pleasing landscape and reduced maintenance. The plants are divided into Common Garden Plants and Native Plants. Some, such as Rudbeckia, are on both lists. It is perfectly acceptable to combine plants from these lists. Chapter 6 offers some suggestions for combinations of plantings to harmonize with several different styles and situations.

This lawn is graded to facilitate sheet flow run off. Water is dispersed over a large area preventing a buildup of velocity, which in turn prevents washouts. This is an effective way of moving water toward a rain garden or in this case the surrounding meadow and woodland.
Credit: Laura Miller RLA

Lenten Rose, Ferns, and Heartleaved Forget-me-not are among the foliage textures that keep this garden interesting through the summer. In addition to remaining attractive through most of the year, these plants love to soak up the excess water.

All this research and planning may seem like a lot of trouble for a small rain garden in your backyard, but the effort will be justified by the resulting improvement in storm water management on your property and the satisfaction of taking positive action toward a better environment. So now you have the seven basic steps toward creating your rain garden. The next chapters will give you more tools to get started.

Sizing the rain garden to handle the drainage on a typical residential property is more of an art than a science. While the system outlined here will handle most situations, if you are concerned about severe drainage problems it is wise to consult a professional for more precise analysis.

The first step is to determine the drainage area. Measure driveways, walks, terraces, pool surrounds, roof, and lawn areas. If you have a scaled plot plan you can save some legwork by using the measurements indicated on the drawing. Do not include mulched beds, meadow, or heavily planted areas in your calculation.

Here's how:

Length of roof multiplied by width of roof
    equals _____

Length of paved areas multiplied by width
    of paved areas equals _____

Length of lawn areas multiplied by width
    of lawn areas equals _____

The sum of the three equations =
    Total drainage area

Step two, determine soil type by observation. Is it gritty with individual particles you can see? Does a handful of damp soil disintegrate when you open your hand? Then it is most likely a sand soil. Are the particles fine, but still distinct? Does damp soil hold its form temporarily when you open your hand, then crumble as you shake it a bit? Then the soil may be silty or a sandy loam. Is the soil smooth and elastic when damp and very hard when dry? Does a handful of it permanently retain its shape when you open your hand? These are characteristics of a clay soil. Clay soil will require a larger area to manage surface water. Some areas of clay soil may not be suitable for a rain garden.

The most common proportions of soil amendents for a rain garden are 1/3 by volume of builders sand and 1/3 organic material such as compost, leaf mold or fine shredded mulch mixed with 1/3 of soil excavated from the garden site. Mix the components thoroughly before backfilling the garden.

There are exceptions to these proportions. A very sandy soil would not benefit from the addition of more sand so it would be mixed in a ratio of 1/3 organic material to 2/3 sandy soil excavated from the site. For a heavy soil such as a clay-loam, increasing the proportion of amendants will not be as beneficial as adding coarser textured material to increase porosity of the soil. For example a fine gravel could be substituted for the builders sand and shredded mulch could be used for the organic component. The proportions of 1/3 excavated soil to 1/3 aggregate and 1/3 organic material would remain the same. Fresh topsoil can also be imported to create the rain garden soil mixture. In my experience, importing topsoil is comparable to importing weeds, so do so with caution.

The next step is to determine the degree of slope on the land. To do so you must set up a series of stakes and lines to allow you to measure the drop in elevation for each 10 feet of length. A line level is helpful for insuring accuracy. A friend with electronic surveying equipment is even more helpful. Some plot plans or construction surveys indicate elevations.

A gently sloping area is preferred. If the grade is more than a drop of 10 feet over a distance of 100 feet and you have no other choice of location, consult a design professional. A flat lot may require regrading with the possible addition of more soil to direct water to the rain garden. Water also can be collected in a drain and piped into the rain garden.

Next find out if your soil will allow water to percolate through to lower layers in a reasonable time period. Dig a hole 6 to 8 inches in diameter and about 24 inches deep. A post hole digger or an auger works well for this. Mark a depth of 12 inches on the side of the hole with marking paint. Fill to 12 inches with water. If the water drains out within 10 minutes the soil is sandy. If it drains within an hour or two the soil is a loamy blend. If it takes more than 24 hours to drain out, the area is not well suited to a rain garden. Try moving to a different spot or consult a design professional with water management expertise.

Armed with these observations and measurements you can begin to calculate the size of your rain garden. The rain garden should be fifteen to twenty percent as large as the area it drains. The smaller figure is adequate if the soil is sandy or silt loam or if the areas to be drained are largely lawn and plant beds. A slope over 6 percent will allow for a slightly smaller and deeper excavation. The larger area will be needed for heavier soils and for draining mostly roofs, driveways and other impermeable surfaces.

Here's how:

Total drainage area multiplied by .15 = Sand soil rain garden area

Total drainage area multiplied by .20 = Silt loam soil rain garden area

Total drainage area multiplied by .25 = Clay/loam rain garden area

Depending upon your house and lawn area, the ideally sized rain garden may be very large. Remember, any effort to conserve water is better than none, so don't be discouraged. Use your best judgment in sizing a rain garden that you can afford to install and manage.

The Unintended Pond

When my friends Bill and Sandy bought a new house, one of the features they enjoyed was a comfortable basement office. It was bright, roomy, and cool during the scorching days of summer, cozy during the winter months. The home's landscaping was minimal and what little there was consisted of sparsely planted raised beds supported by rotting timbers. With the effort of moving in and redecorating, they didn't give the landscape much thought at first. What they failed to observe was the fact that the back yard had taken on characteristics of a swamp with soggy soil and standing water in low areas. Then they got 6 inches of rain one spring day and their sump pump was overwhelmed. In just two hours the basement office was flooded. It took nearly two months to return it to an efficient workspace.

In talking to their neighbors they found they weren't alone. Every one of them had encountered problems with frequently flooded basements and soggy lawns. Nearby Marsh Road was probably named for the natural condition of the area. As experienced do-it-yourselfers they decided to correct the water problem with a rain garden. After some research they designed the garden for their small property. For good measure they added a Japanese dry pond to catch any overflow, rather than risk having it run onto the neighboring properties.

They added soil to raise the grade around the house foundation and graded the remaining property to flow toward the rain garden. In the space marked out as the rain garden, the soil was excavated. It was mixed with builder's sand and compost in a ratio of 1/3 each sand, compost, and soil. The dry pond was excavated to twelve inches at the center and lined with large river washed stones. Excess soil was incorporated into berms surrounding the rain garden and dry pond. The finished rain garden and dry pond looked perfect … and then it rained some more.

Stormwater from the downspouts, sump pump, and surrounding landscape was channeled into dry pond as planned. However, the water did not percolate into the soil and dissipate. Instead the dry pond became a full pond. A heavy clay sub-soil sealed the basin so securely that the only loss of water came from evaporation. Toads soon arrived and laid their eggs. Tadpoles hatched and matured into more toads. Realizing that the pond was there to stay, they added mosquito control, beneficial bacteria, and water plants. Algae bloomed and a solution to that problem was found.

While surrounded by a rain garden, this "pond" has become a reservoir for runoff. Sometimes called a dew pond, it receives any nutrients applied to the lawn or garden as well as runoff from surrounding paved and roofed areas so it shares many of the problems of modern waterways. In addition this pond has the disadvantage of no natural water movement or cleansing processes. The only water renewal comes with rainfall or watering of adjacent lawn and beds. Since water does not percolate into their soil, my friends have two choices. They can treat the pond with mechanical aeration and filtration or they can fill it in with a soil mix and convert it to a bog garden. This surprise pond could have been avoided by soil analysis, careful research, and design.

Chapter 5
Rain Garden Plants

"Everyone understands that water is essential to life. But many are only just now beginning to grasp how essential it is to everything in life – food, energy, transportation, nature, leisure, identity, culture, social norms, and virtually all the products used on a daily basis."
World Business Council for Sustainable Development (WBCSD)

Plants are a significant ally in the effort to conserve water. As we discussed earlier they contribute in many ways to a healthy water balance. The destruction of plants results in upset of the hydrologic cycle and the loss of productive land and waterways to erosion, pollution, and, in extreme cases, desertification. The soils bordering waterways are referred to as "riparian," that is soils that are very wet or flooded sometimes and dry at others. Wet mesic refers to upland soils that are often wet but not flooded.

Riparian plantings, those occurring near waterways, are common to ponds edges, bogs, and wetlands. They thrive in rain gardens. These plants will tolerate excessive moisture at times. There are other plants, beyond those listed, that may thrive in riparian or wet mesic conditions typical of the rain garden. I have listed those that are most readily available. While most of them will thrive over much of the United States, some of those listed may not be hardy in your locale.

Although I have not listed plants known to be extremely invasive, be forewarned that native plants have evolved to survive in harsh growing conditions. Given the favorable conditions of prepared soil and plentiful moisture, some of them will grow rampantly. That can be both a benefit and a problem. If you don't mind ruthlessly weeding out seedlings or plants that spread by stolons, you may enjoy the luxuriant growth of a plant that crowds out weeds and requires little additional effort to maintain. On the other hand, if you want a more controlled appearance, some of these native plants may become your weeds. It is always wise to do some independent research. Check with local nurserymen, your university extension service, or visit a nearby botanic garden. Many courses on native plants are available today. A visit to an example garden at a university or public garden is advised.

If you are attempting to keep maintenance to a minimum, select dense, compact shrubs, and under plant them with a ground cover such as American cranberry or Lilyturf. The shrubs will fill the area and shade soil while the ground cover will assist in preventing weed growth. Match plants to the conditions of light, PH, wind exposure, and soil texture in your garden.

The rich colors of native meadow flowers glow in the fading light of a late summer day. *Credit: Prairie Moon Nursery*

These plants can be found in local nurseries and garden centers, mail order catalogues, and on the internet. If your budget is tight you can start many perennials from seed. With care, dozens of plants can be produced from a $3.00 seed packet. It does take time and patience and a willingness to nurse young plants along until they are sturdy enough to be planted in the rain garden. Sources of plants can be found on page 94.

Native Plants

Flowering Perennials

Acoris calamus Sweet Flag
Actea rubra Baneberry or Dolls eyes
Allium cerynum Nodding Onion
Amopha fruticosa False Indigo
Angelica atropurpurea Angelica
Aruncus dioicus Goatsbeard
Aster nova-angeliae-New England Aster
Asclepias incarnata, Swamp Milkweed
Baptisia australis Blue False Indigo
Boltonia asteroides False Aster
Caltha palustris Marsh Marigold
Camassia scilloides Wild Hyacinth
Campanula americana Tall Bellflower
Chelone lyonii, False Turtlehead
Clematis virginiana Virgin's Bower (vine)
Dodeocathon anystinum Shooting Star
Eupatorium coelestinum Blue Mist Flower
Eupatorium maculatum, Joe-pye Weed
Filipendula rubra Queen of the Prairie
Geum triflorum Prairie Smoke
Helianthus angustifolius Swamp sunflower
Helenium autumnale Sneeze Weed
Hibiscus palustris Swamp Rose Mallow
Hypericum virginicum Marsh St. John's Wort
Iris prismatica Slender Blue Flag
Iris pseudocorus Yellow Flag Iris
Iris versicolor Blue Flag Iris
Iris virginiana Wild Blue Iris
Liatris spicata Blazing Star
Lilium philadelphinum Prairie Lily
Lobelia cardinalis, Cardinal Flower
Lobelia syphilitica, Blue Lobelia
Mertensia virginica Virginia Blue Bells
Monarda didyma, Oswego Tea
Monarda fistula Wild Bergamont
Phlox diveracata Wild Blue Phlox
Phlox pilosa Prairie Phlox
Polemonium reptans Jacobs Ladder
Rudbeckia hirts Common Black Eyed Susan
Rudbeckia maxima Great Coneflower
Rudbeckia triloba Browneyed Susan
Silene stellata Starry Campion
Silphium perfoliatum Cup Plant
Smilacina racemosa Solomon's Plume
Solidago gigantea Late Goldenrod
Uvularia grandiflora Lady Bells
Veronicastrum virginiacum Culvers Root
Vernonia noveboracensis, Common Ironweed
Viola papilionacea Common Blue Violet

Pale mauve Swamp Milkweed blends with any color and is sure to draw every butterfly in the neighborhood to your garden.

An emerald island of Little Bluestem and Quaking Grass work overtime in taking up excess moisture. These are undemanding plants that will do their best to thrive under adverse conditions and they add interest to the fall and winter garden with their bright tan foliage and interesting seed heads.

Stately Joe Pye Weed Eupatorium maculatum attracts butterflies and beneficial insects to the garden. *Credit: Prairie Moon Nursery*

Royal purple Iron Weed Vernonia novaboracensis is anything but a weed. It is a reliable, large scale, stalwart of a rain garden, damp meadow or native planting. *Credit: Prairie Moon Nursery*

A lovely forest dweller, Flowering Raspberry enjoys a moist shaded environment where it will happily provide lovely blue green foliage and raspberry pink flowers, but don't expect any fruit. Birds quickly consume the raspberry-like berries.

Brilliant Cardinal Flower is first cousin to the subtler Meadow Lobelia. The Lobelias will reproduce themselves if allowed to set seed.

Blue Meadow Lobelia is a late summer blooming member of a distinguished swamp dwelling family.

Ferns

Adiantum pedatum Maiden Hair Fern
Athyrium filix-femina, Lady fern
Onoclea sensibilis Sensitive Fern
Osmunda regalis, Royal fern
Osmunda cinnamomea, Cinnamon fern
Polypodium vulgare Common polypody

Grasses and Sedges

Andropogen gerardii Giant Bluestem
Calamagrostis canadensis Blue Joint Grass
Carex pendula, Drooping sedge
Carex stipata, Tussock sedge
Carex pennsylvanica
Carex stricta
Carex morrowii'Silver Sceptre'
Elymus canadensis Wild Rye
Glyceria maxima var. variegata Variegated
   manna grass
Juncus canadensis Canada Rush
Juncus effusus Common Rush
Muhlenbergia glomerata Marsh Muhley Grass
Panicum virgatum Switch Grass,
   cv. 'North Wind' 'Prairie Wind'
Scirpus cyperinus Wool Grass
Spartinia pectinata Cord Grass
Spartina Patens Salt Hay
Sporbus heterolepsis Northern Dropseed
Stipa giganteus
Uniola latifolia River Oats
Zizania aquatica Canada wild rice

Shade loving and reliable
the wild Geranium Geranium
maculatum and Sensitive Fern
Onoclea sensibilis combine
well in the rain garden. *Credit:*
Prairie Moon Nursery

Contrasting textures
of Northern Dropseed
Sporbus heterolep-
sis and Cup Plant
Silphium perfoliatum
create an attractive
and carefree combi-
nation. *Credit: Prairie*
Moon Nursery

The lovely pink flower of Rose Mallow contrasts with purple Ironweed in a sunny, rain garden.

Switch Grass is equally at home in the moist soil of a rain garden, in near desert conditions, or growing along a super-highway. One of our most durable and adaptable ornamental grasses, it is a graceful presence in the garden from summer through late winter. Several cultivars have been developed sporting reddish flowers or silvery blue green foliage.

A large shrub or small tree Elderberry bears lacey panicles of creamy flowers followed by shiny black berries that are relished by birds. A sunny rain garden is the perfect spot for this hardy, fruiting plant. Its flowers may be coated with batter and deep-fried and its berries are used for tart jams, jellies, and pies.

Native Trees and Shrubs

Acre rubrum, Red Maple
Amelanchier laevis, Shadbush
Asimina triloba, Pawpaw
Betula nigra, River birch
Cephalanthus occidentalis, Buttonbush
Chionanthus virginicus Fringe Tree
Clethra alnifolia, Sweet pepperbush
Cornus amomum, Silky dogwood
Cornus stolonifera, Red osier dogwood
Fothergilla gardenii, Dwarf fothergilla
Ilex glabra Inkberry Holly
Ilex verticillata, Winterberry Holly
Lindera benzoin, Spicebush
Liquidambar styraciflua, Sweet gum
Magnolia Virginiana Sweetbay Magnolia
Myrica pensylvanica Northern Bayberry
Prunus pumila Eastern Sand Cherry
Rosa carolina Prairie Rose
Rosa palustris Swamp Rose
Salix lucida Shining Willow
Sambucus canadensis, American elderberry
Thuja occidentalis Eastern Arborvitae
Viburnum dentatum, Arrowwood Viburnum

The flowers of Cup Plant, soar above the garden. They are surrounded by the usual complement of butterflies. Small birds are also attracted to the plant for both water, held in its stem clasping leaves, and seeds.

Winterberry is the undisputed star of the Winter garden. Its bold red berries brighten the darkest day, look spectacular against a backdrop of evergreens or snow, and last until emerging leaves crowd them out in the spring.

My favorite, Siberian Iris, Caesar's Brother, is garden royalty with sturdy stalks of bright purple flowers. It isn't the longest blooming plant, but the late spring show it puts on makes it worth waiting for. Foliage remains nice all season once the flower stalks are cut back.

Cammasia is a native wetland plant valued for its late spring flowers. Bulbs were a food source of early Native Americans. Credit: Prairie Moon Nursery

Oranges, reds, purples, and pinks— cheerful Daylilies come in a broad range of warm colors and blends. Reliable and pest free, they put on an amazing show in the garden. The only downside to daylilies is that they need to be cut back after blooming when their foliage becomes unattractive—a small price for a plant that literally knocks itself out blooming.

Common Garden Plants

Flowering Perennials

Acorus calamus 'Variegatus' Variegated sweet flag
Astilbe arendsii and chinensis False Spirea
Astilboides tabularis Rogersia
Brunnera macrophylla Perennial Forget-me-not
Calla palustris Bog Arum
Campanula lactifolia Milky Bellflower
Geranium 'Johnson's Blue' Johnson's Blue hardy geranium
Gunnera manicata
Helleborus niger Christmas Rose
Helleborus orientalis Lenten Rose
Helleborus hybrids Hybrid Hellebors
Hemerocallis Many varieties Daylily
Hosta-many varieties Plantain Lily
Iris laevigata Water iris
Iris ensata Japanese iris
Iris siberica Siberian Iris
Liriope muscari Lilyturf
Ligularia clivorum 'Desdemona' Big Leaf Ligularia
Ligularia dentate Ragwort
Lilium superbum Turk's Cap Lily
Leucojum aestivum Summer snowflake
Lysamachia nummularia 'Aurea' Golden creeping jenny
Lysamachia puncata Yellow loosestrife
Myosotis sylvestris Woodland Forget-me-not
Omphlodes cappadocica Creeping Forget-me-not
Petasites japonicus Japanese Butterbur
Primula japonica Japanese or candelabra primrose
Ranunculus ficaria 'Floro Pleno' Yellow Buttercup

Ferns

Mattueuccia struthiopteris Ostrich fern

Grasses and sedges

Carex elata 'Bowles Golden' Golden tufted Sedge
Chasmanthium latifolia Northern Sea Oats
Darmera peltata Umbrella Plant
Euphorbia palustris Wood spurge
Juncus effuses spiralis Corkscrew Rush
Miscanthus sinensis 'Gracillimus' Maiden Grass
Miscanthus sinensis 'Zebrinus' Zebra Grass
Pennesitum alopecuroides Fountain Grass
Pennesitum japonicum 'Karley rose' Rose Fountain Grass
Phalaris arundinacae Ribbon Grass

The papery remains of a hydrangea bloom again with a blossom of snow.

Lady Fern is one of many woodland dwellers that enjoy the damp soil of a rain garden. Most fern species prefer a shaded garden to look their best.

Rudbeckia 'Goldstrum' is a bright spot of long-lasting sunshine in the summer garden. The only requirement this reliable plant has is sufficient levels of moisture. With a layer of mulch, established plants do not require supplemental watering and they will happily crowd weeds out of your garden. Left to mature the button like seed heads are attractive all winter and provide a food source for birds.

Liriope "Big Blue" is one of the best ground covers for any garden soil. In full sun the foliage will be a lighter green and require higher moisture levels. In damp, shaded situations its strap-like leaves are a glossy dark green throughout the winter. It needs a haircut in early spring and very little else in the way of maintenance.

A wonderful combination of Geranium 'Johnson's Blue' and Lady's Mantle are both hardy, moisture loving plants that work well in the cottage garden or anywhere a splash of long blooming color is needed. Geraniums are robust garden performers that come in a range of cool pinks, purples, and mauves as well as white and a coral pink cultivar. Do not confuse hardy perennial Geranium with Pelargoniums, which are often sold as container and bedding plants and commonly called Geraniums.

Red Twig Dogwood is attractive during the summer with
its fresh green leaves and creamy white flowers. In late
summer it bears bluish berries that are quickly consumed
by birds. In winter this plant really shines with its bright
red branches. To retain its bright color, Red Twig Dogwood
needs to be cut back severely in spring. Only new growth
sports glowing red twigs. In the background is an Inkberry
Holly, a native evergreen.

Trees and Shrubs

Acer palmatum Japanese Maple
Aesculus parviflora Bottlebrush Buckeye
Alnus incana 'Laciniata' Cut leaved alder
Betula nigra 'Heritage'
Betula occidentalis Water Birch
Cornus alba 'Siberica' Siberian Dogwood
Cornus florida cultivars Hybrid Dogwood
Cornus sericea Coral stem dogwood
Corylus maxima 'Purpurea' Purple leaved Hazel
Clethra 'Ruby Spice' Ruby Spice Summersweet
Hydrangea many varieties
Kalmia latifolia Mountain Laurel
Magnolia grandiflora Southern or Bullbay Magnolia
Metasequoia glyptostroboides Dawn Redwood
Salix alba 'Britzensis' Coral stem Willow
Salix chrysocoma Golden Weeping Willow
Salix matsudana 'Tortuosa' Contorted willow
Taxodium distichum Bald Cypress
Vaccinum macroparpon American Cranberry

Other Plants of Interest

These plants are not hardy in all parts of the United States. They need to be dug and overwintered in a cool place.

Canna spp. Canna lily
Crinum Americanum Robustum American Bog Lily
Zantedeschia aethiopica Calla lily

The 'Heritage' River Birch is a real focal point with its beautiful peeling bark in shades of tan. A groundcover of Liriope is a perfect foil for the interesting texture and color of the bark. A graceful, fast growing, tree with clear yellow fall color, the River Birch does not share the disease and insect problems Birches are known for.

The Hybrid Sunflower 'Lemon Queen' is a plant for the large border or meadow. Spreading slowly from the base as well as seeding freely, it blooms from mid-summer into fall with clear yellow flowers that are excellent for cutting. Like all sunflowers, its seeds are a nourishing food source for birds.

Hydrangea is a water loving cultivar of coarse textured shrubs. Most Hydrangeas prefer some relief from mid-day sun, but they will survive in full sun given enough moisture. They bring a welcome touch of mid-summer color in a cool palette of blues, violets, pinks, and white. Long lasting papery flowers change colors as they age, turning to attractive shades of Old Rose or Lime Green.

Gunnera or Giant Rhubarb is not for the faint of heart or the small garden. Giant Rhubarb is undemanding except for its prodigious space requirement and high moisture requirement. It spreads slowly from rootstock and its gigantic leaves reach 2 to 3 feet across held on sturdy stems as tall as 6 feet.

Switch Grass or Panicum virgatum
is willing to grow anywhere under
almost any conditions, wet or dry.
It does prefer at least six hours of
sun a day. Here it blends with the
textures and colors of flowering
perennials and grasses.

Native Flowers for the Rain Garden

Native flowers come in a wide range of colors and forms. Here is a small sampling of those listed to help you see the many possibilities offered by natives.

Ironweed Vernonia novaborencsis
Credit: Prairie Moon Nursery

Nodding Onion Allium cerynum
Credit: Prairie Moon Nursery

Angelica *Angelica atropurpurea*
Credit: Prairie Moon Nursery

New England Aster *Aster nova-angeliae*
Credit: Prairie Moon Nursery

Swamp Milkweed *Asclepias incarnata*
Credit: Prairie Moon Nursery

Joe Pye Weed *Eupatoreum maculatum*
Credit: Prairie Moon Nursery

Shooting Star *Dodeocathon anystinum*
Credit: Prairie Moon Nursery

Queen of the Prairie *Filipendula rubra*
Credit: Prairie Moon Nursery

Prairie Smoke *Geum triflorum*
Credit: Prairie Moon Nursery

Oswego Tea *Monarda Didyma*
Credit: Prairie Moon Nursery

Jacobs Ladder *Polemonium reptans*
Credit: Prairie Moon Nursery

Wild Hyacinth *Camassia scilloides*
Credit: Prairie Moon Nursery

Wild Blue Iris *Iris virginica*
Credit: Prairie Moon Nursery

Wild Blue Violet *Viola papilonacea*
Credit: Prairie Moon Nursery

Starry Campion *Silene stellata*
Credit: Prairie Moon Nursery

Virginia Bluebells *Merten-sia virginica Credit: Prairie Moon Nursery*

Cardinal Flower *Lobelia cardinalis Credit: Prairie Moon Nursery*

Browneyed Susan *Rudbeckia triloba Credit: Prairie Moon Nursery*

Solomon's Plume *Smilacina racemosa Credit: Prairie Moon Nursery*

Culver's Root *Veronicastrum virginicum Credit: Prairie Moon Nursery*

Chapter 6
Pleasing Plant Combinations

*S*elect plants carefully when planning your rain garden. Do enough research to be sure they are hardy in your USDA zone. Select for plants that tolerate widely fluctuating levels of soil moisture. Check heights and widths of plants at maturity to avoid overcrowding and wasting time, effort, and money by planting too many plants. Repeating a few plants will result in attractive masses of color and a more satisfactory picture than single specimens of a large variety of plants.

When planning your plantings, start by selecting a small tree or large shrub, two or three small to mid-sized shrubs, and twenty to thirty perennials for a small residential rain garden. Try to include some evergreen plants and a variety of heights and interesting flowers and foliage. Add a ground cover and you should have an attractive and thriving garden that will require little maintenance when it becomes established. For those with limited plant experience, I have suggested some planting combinations below. For a larger garden, increase the numbers of each plant or add more variety to your planting plan. These garden plans are not meant to be copied. They are designed to start you thinking about plant combinations. However, if one of them appeals to you, by all means use it for your rain garden. For more information on each plant go to www.plants.usda.gov.

A cultivated meadow. In the foreground is Rudbeckia hirta, The Blackeyed Susan, Daylily, Hosta, Milkweed, and Aster foliage. In the background is the glossy, evergreen foliage of Bullbay Magnolia.

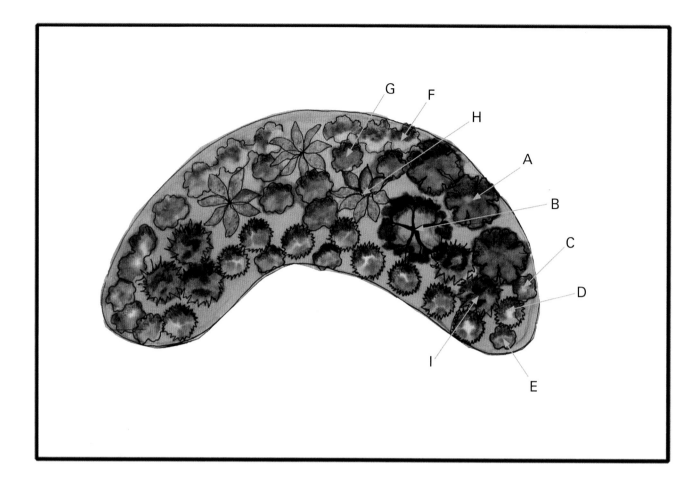

An Easy, Colorful Rain Garden

A. 3 *Ilex glabra 'Shamrock'* or 'Compacta' Shamrock or Compact Inkberry
B. 1 *Ilex verticillata 'Winter Red'* or "Winter Red" Winterberry
C. 5 *Uvularia grandiflora* or Lady Bells
D. 10 *Hemerocallis 'Happy Returns'* or Happy Returns Daylily
E. 5 *Brunnera macrophylla* or Perennial Forget-me-not
F. 6 *Eupatorium coelestinum 'Blue Mist'* or Blue Mist Fleeceflower
G. 7 *Chelone glabra* or False Turtlehead
H. 3 *Hosta 'Sum and Substance'* or Sum and Substance' Hosta
I. 5 *Iris Siberica 'Ceasar's Brother'* or Ceasar's Brother Siberian Iris

This free form garden is appropriate for an area in full sun or very light shade such as that cast by high overhead limbs. Spring gets a warm welcome from clear blue Forget-me-nots and creamy yellow Lady Bells. Next, Siberian Iris proudly displays a multitude of royal purple blossoms. Siberian Iris is a totally dependable and carefree plant. The foliage is attractive much of the year with a graceful, grass-like texture. It turns a pleasing gold color in fall.

Daylily 'Happy Return's sports lively clear yellow blooms throughout the summer. The dramatic chartreuse foliage of Hosta 'Sum and Substance' is a perfect foil for seasonal flowers and it contributes pale lilac spikes in late summer just before the pink False Turtlehead and Blue Mist Fleece Flower decorate the garden for autumn. Red berries and evergreen leaves warm the picture throughout the winter months.

Winterberry's bold red display stands out against an evergreen background of Inkberry. Winterberry may require a pollinator. I recommend waiting a full season to see if it sets berries. If there are other Winterberries growing and berrying in your neighborhood, yours will most likely berry freely. This garden is an example of mixing native and common garden plants. All are easy care, pest free, and colorful.

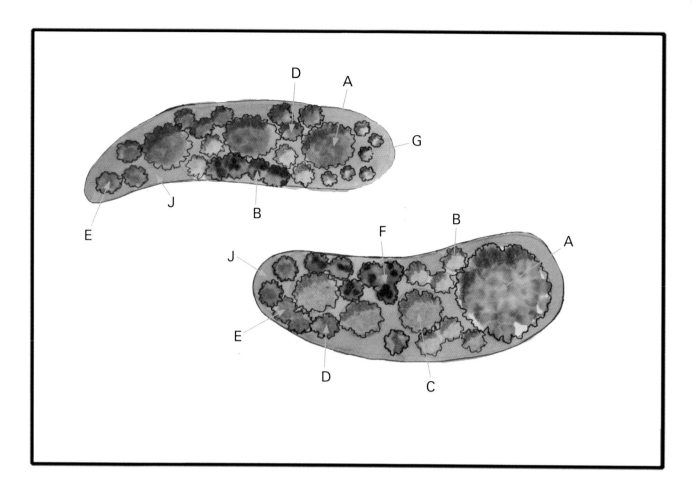

A Shady Rain Garden

A. 1 *Chionanthus virginicus* or White Fringe Tree
B. 10 *Athyrium felix-femina* or Lady Fern
C. 3 *Hosta seiboldiana* or Seibolds Blue Hosta
D. 10 *Geranium maculatum* or Cranesbill Geranium
E. 5 *Helleborus hybrida* or Christmas Rose
F. 10 *Astilbe arendsii* or False Spirea
G. 6 *Brunnera macrophylla* or Heartleaved Forget-me-not
H. 3 *Fothergilla gardenii* or Dwarf Fothergilla
J. 32 plugs *Lysamachia nummularia* or Creeping Jennie Ground Cover

This shade planting scheme is appropriate for a garden beneath high overhanging tree limbs or one that is shaded by a structure during the afternoon hours. It provides an interesting range of foliage textures and shades of green through the growing season with intermittent flowering from earliest spring.

Fringe tree is a small scale tree with delightfully fragrant flowers in spring. Dwarf Fothergilla soon follows suit with honey scented, white, bottlebrush-like flowers. It also contributes beautiful fall foliage of red, orange, and gold. The heart-leaved Forget-me-nots are a lovely clear blue over a long bloom time in spring. Allow them to go to seed for masses of these sky blue flowers.

Cranesbill Geranium is a very easy care, dependable garden plant that will reward you with masses of mauve single blossoms in summer. Astilbe is another summer bloomer, which comes in red, shades of pink, mauve, or clear white. Lime green Lady Fern and blue foliaged Seiboldi Hostas provide a lovely contrast and the hostas throw up spikes of white flowers in late summer. The Lenten Rose's papery flowers appear in late winter and persist through early summer. Their lovely evergreen foliage enlivens the winter garden. Creeping Jennie is a fast growing, but not invasive ground cover that loves to soak up all the water it can get. It is fine textured and will not fight with other flowering plants. It also flowers with yellow buttercup-like flowers that are all but hidden in the lush foliage creeping through the garden.

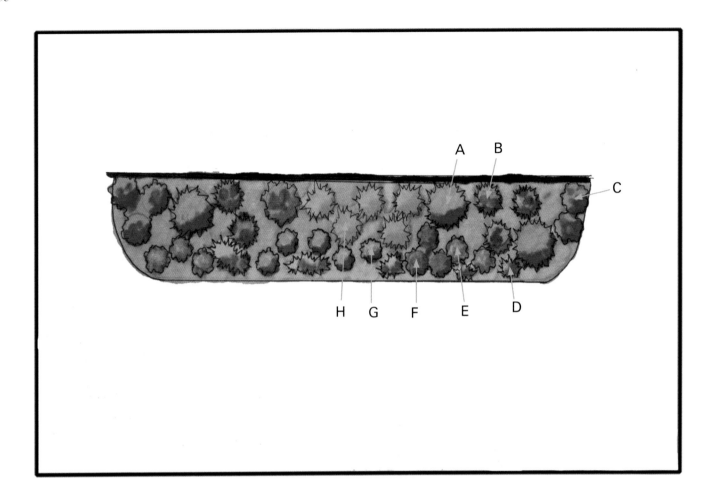

A Meadow Rain Garden Border for Full Sun

A. 3 *Juniperus virginiana* or Eastern Red Cedar
B. 5 *Panicum virgatum 'Hans Hermes'* or Hans Hermes Red Switch Grass
C. 5 *Vernonia novaborincensis* or Ironweed
D. 9 *Uniola latifolia* or Sea oats
E. 3 *Rudbeckia triloba* or Brown-eyed Susan
F. 3 *Aster nova angelia* or New England Aster
G. 5 *Solidago sempervirans* or Goldenrod
H. 5 *Andropogon gerardii* or Big Bluestem
I. 1 *Eupatorium maculatum* or Joe Pye Weed

A large, informal area can be covered by this exuberant meadow planting. It will be attractive year around with lush grasses and meadow flowers contrasting with the upright form and evergreen foliage of the Red Cedars. The meadow will be a bit slow to develop in spring since meadow grasses enjoy warm weather. Late summer will find the garden alive with fluttering wings visiting Joe Pye Weed and Brown-eyed Susan. In early fall Goldenrod will provide landing fields of golden fleece for bees and butterflies. Ironweed's noble purple heads will rise above it all to end the growing season.

Red Cedar's bluish berries attract many varieties of birds, including bluebirds and cedar waxwings. Its evergreen foliage also provides secure nesting sites for many birds. Swaying grasses and tall meadow flowers attract birds and butterflies in summer and remain visually interesting all winter. For a larger meadow rain garden, mechanical application of a wet mesic seed mixture is recommended. Establishing a meadow from seed can be challenging and an expert should be consulted.

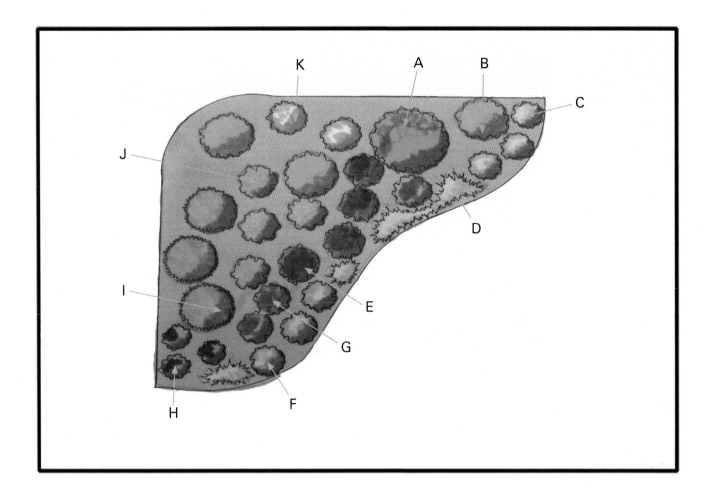

A Wildlife Habitat Rain Garden

A. 1 *Viburnum dentatum 'Blue Jay'* or 'Blue Blaze' Arrowwood Viburnum
B. 3 *Ilex glabra 'Shamrock'* or 'Compacta' Shamrock or Compact Inkberry
C. 3 *Rudbeckia trifoliata* or Brown-eyed Susan
D. 9 *Uniola latifolia* or Seaoats
E. 4 *Monarda didyma* or Scarlet Bee Balm
F. 3 *Coreopsis lanceolata* or Lanceleaf Tickseed
G. 3 *Asclepias incarnata* or Swamp Milkweed
H. 3 *Lobelia cardinalis* Cardinal Flower
I. 3 *Panicum virgatum 'North Wind'* or North Wind Switch Grass
J. 4 *Solidago sempervirans* or Goldenrod
K. 2 *Silphium perfoliatum* or Cup Plant

This planting will provide food and cover to attract a variety of wildlife. Add a water source such as a birdbath, small pond, or fountain and place a garden bench or chair nearby to enjoy the parade of birds and butterflies feeding here. Both the Viburnum and the Inkberry provide nourishing blue-black berries for birds and their dense foliage affords secure nesting sites.

Cup plant holds water in its leaf axials for small birds and insects to take a sip. Its masses of yellow daisies, held high on 6- to 8-foot stems, produce nutritious seeds as does the Brown-eyed Susan and Switch Grass. The large scaled Cup Plant is not for the faint of heart, but it is carefree and hardy and it presents a lovely picture silhouetted against a blue sky.

Scarlet Bee Balm and Cardinal flower attract hummingbirds while Goldenrod and soft mauve Swamp Milkweed will be aflutter with butterflies in late summer. With the addition of a water source, this garden will qualify for certification by the National Wildlife Federation as a wildlife habitat.

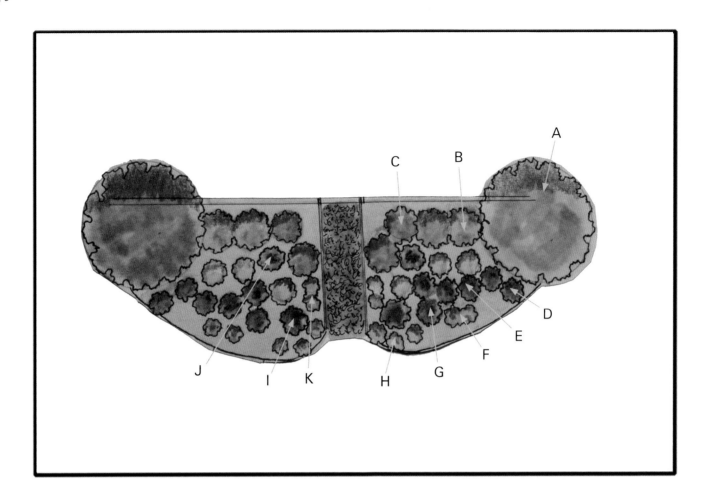

A Cottage Border Rain Garden

A. 2 *Magnolia virginiana* or Sweetbay Magnolia
B. 4 *Clethera alnifolia 'Rosea'* or Rose Summer Sweet
C. 4 *Hibiscus palustris* or Rose Mallow
D. 6 *Liatris spicata* or Blazing Star
E. 6 *Aruncus dioscious* or Goatsbeard
F. 4 *Campanula lactiflora* or Milky Bellflower
G. 6 *Lobelia siphilitica Meadow* or Giant Blue Lobelia
H. 6 *Phlox pilosa* or Downy Phlox
I. 2 *Monarda didyma* or Scarlet Bee Balm
J. 2 *Aster nove angliae* or New England Aster
K. 4 *Omphlodes cappadocica* or Creeping Forget-me-not

This is a colorful planting reminiscent of old fashioned cottage gardens. It will keep blooming throughout the summer, providing cut flowers and attracting complements from your neighbors. If a cottage garden suits your taste, you could add a white picket fence or a rose arch to enhance the style. This garden will attract butterflies and hummingbirds as they visit for a sip of nectar.

The sketch shows this garden as mirror image borders, intersected by a pea gravel path and backed by a fence. The size and shape can be modified to fit any sunny space.

In early summer the garden begins blooming with Phlox pilosa and Milky Bellflower. Sweetbay Magnolia is a native tree that blooms intermittently through the summer with creamy cup shaped flowers that emit a delicious lemony perfume.

During the warmest months Summer Sweet competes for the most delightful fragrance from its spikes of rose pink blossoms. The Rose Mallow or Swamp Hibiscus blooms during the summer with silky, funnel shaped, pink, flowers often with a red blotch in the throat. Interesting seedpods follow as blooms fade. White Goats beard stands tall in mid-summer along with Blue Meadow Lobelia and Scarlet Bee Balm. Mauve Liatris blazes in late summer and New England Aster ends the season with a mass of bright purple.

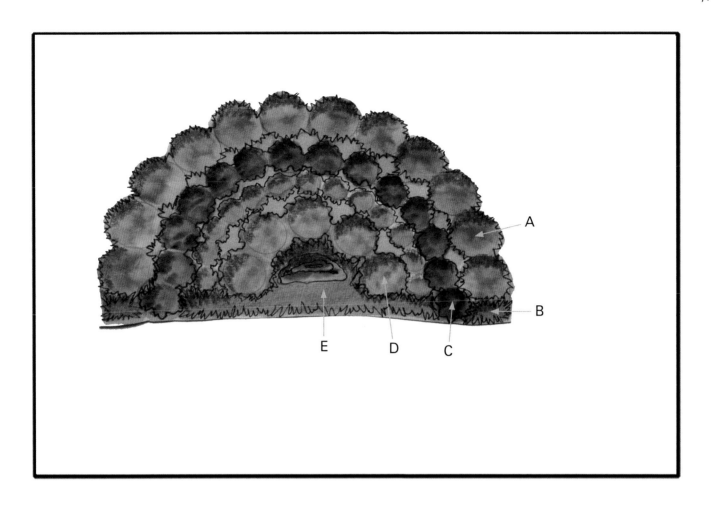

A Formal Rain Garden

A. 12 *Juniperus virginiana 'Princeton Sentry'* or Princeton Sentry Cedar
B. 36 *Liriope muscari 'Big Blue'* or Big Blue Liriope
C. 14 *Ilex glabra 'Compacta'* or Compact Inkberry
D. 5 *Hydrangea 'Nikko Blue'* or Nikko Blue Hydrangea
E. 20 *Boltonia astroides 'Snowbank'* or Snowbank Boltonia

This symmetrical and refined planting could also be arranged as a long border to catch run-off and provide screening of views and privacy. They can also be grouped to surround a piece of sculpture as shown here, or a bench or fountain to create a very personal setting. Eastern Red Cedars cultivar "Princeton Sentry" is recommended for uniformity. The evergreen foliage provides cover and food for many birds.

Inkberry can be clipped for a uniform, formal appearance or left to develop its natural billowing form. Tall growing Boltonia blooms in fall with a flurry of snow-white flowers to contrast with the shades of green. Blue Hydranges blooms through-out summer and its cool mounds of color create a wonderful backdrop for the focal point. Liriope is an excellent, low maintenance ground cover that blooms in late summer with refined purple spikes.

Chapter 7
Installing a Rain Garden

"Man is a complex being; he makes deserts bloom and lakes die."

Gil Stern

When you are satisfied with your design, it's time to begin installation. First call your local utility hotline and have gas, water, and electric lines marked in the area to be excavated. Even if you located them at the design phase, have them flagged before you start to dig. The risks of injury or substantial financial liability are worthy of extra precaution.

If you plan on hiring a contractor to install your landscaping, it is important to be sure the people doing the day-to-day work understand the intended outcome. Since this is a relatively new type of garden in many areas, you need to be vigilant so that installation proceeds as planned. If you are doing the installation yourself, consider hiring an excavator for the initial digging, mixing, and backfilling. Moving tons of earth is an unpleasant chore that may result in a sore back or worse.

As a first step, use lime, chalk, or marking paint to draw the outline of the rain garden. Does it look as good on the land as it does on paper? Is the placement correct to catch as much run-off as possible? Are you pleased with the appearance of the rain garden as it relates to the rest of your landscape? If it is not exactly as you envisioned it, now is the time to make changes. When the shape and location are pleasing to you, you are ready to begin the exciting work of creating a rain garden.

Instead of digging out existing lawn or weeds, take time to kill them by spraying them with Roundup®. You could also clear the area organically by covering it with clear plastic, which will cook the vegetation including many rootlets and seeds. The former will allow you to start digging in about twenty-four hours; the latter, which will reduce weed re-growth, will take four to six weeks of summer weather, so it should be done well before you plan to begin installation.

If you have planned a small rain garden, not much more than 200 square feet, and your soil is light, you may want to tackle it with a shovel. In the case of a sandy, well-drained soil, simply excavate the area to a depth of six inches; amend the soil with compost, build the berm, fill the garden leaving a slight depression, plant and mulch. For heavier soil the garden area should be excavated from 12 to 24 inches. If you are confident in your ability to operate such equipment, a small backhoe or power digger may be available from rental centers in your locale. If you are not comfortable with a digging machine, rototilling layer by layer will break up the soil and roots, making hand digging easier. Take care to excavate to the proper depth without exhausting or injuring yourself.

A rain garden border in late summer. Eastern Red Cedar, Winterberry, Goldenrod and ornamental grasses thrive on runoff from paddocks beyond the fence.

For a silt-loam soil, excavate to 12 inches and mix backfill with one-third sand and one-third compost by volume. Fill this mixture to six inches below the surrounding grade, plant, and mulch. Remaining soil may be used to form a berm to retain moisture or to raise low areas and encourage runoff to move toward the rain garden. A heavy clay soil requires the most extreme measures. It should be removed to a depth of two feet and replaced by a mixture of 30 percent sand, 40 percent fresh topsoil, and 30 percent compost to within six inches of the surrounding grade. This is hard, heavy work and I recommend hiring an excavation contractor to do the digging with power equipment. You may wish to have the heavy soil removed from your property and replaced with good topsoil for the berm.

The entire garden should slope slightly toward the center, where water will stand the longest, and that is where the most moisture tolerant plants should be planted. Just inside the perimeter, the rain garden will drain more quickly. Wet meadow plants and many common garden plants will thrive in those conditions. The berm retaining the rain garden should be planted with plants that will tolerate some dryness. A buffer strip of lawn surrounding the rain garden will help to slow runoff and begin filtering out pollutants and particulate matter.

During the design process you will have selected the plants you wish to use in your rain garden. Review your selections to be sure they are suitable both from a cultural and from an aesthetically pleasing standpoint. You may purchase plants from a local garden center, home improvement center, or from a mail order nursery. Gardening friends share perennials by dividing established plants. Environmental agencies and organizations often operate nurseries producing native plants for wetland and riparian restoration. They may provide such plants at economical cost for environmental projects. Please do not collect native plants from the wild. It is against the law in most states and it is destructive of native ecosystems. An exception may be made for an area that is slated for destruction or development. In that case, before you collect check with local authorities to be sure you are not breaking any laws and get permission from landowners before entering private property.

Planting and mulching are the final steps in installing your rain garden. Plants should be planted no deeper than they grew in the pot or nursery. Burying the crowns will kill many plants because roots and stems need air to survive. It is better to plant them a bit higher than they originally grew than to plant them deeper. Loosen and spread roots of pot grown plants. If you are using plugs, it will be easier to mulch before planting, then touch up with a light top dressing. Spread about two inches of mulch over the area to be planted. More is unnecessary and may actually slow the development of some plants. Keep mulch away from the bark of trees and woody shrubs. When piled against the trunk of a tree or shrub, mulch encourages insect, disease, and small mammal damage and may kill your plants. When you've finished planting, a thorough watering prepares your rain garden to grow.

Traditional garden features
such as vine covered overhead
structures and fountains may
be part of a rain garden. In
this example of a sustainable
garden, recycled materials and
pea gravel paving support the
concept of an environmentally
friendly and sustainable garden.

A rain garden brightens an overcast winter day with plantings of Winterberry and Swamp Cypress. It was designed to collect runoff from an expanse of pavement on a college campus.

A dry laid sidewalk allows surface water to percolate through to a reservoir below where it is held until is seeps into deep groundwater channels. Credit: LandStudies Inc.

Who knows what you will encounter when walking this well traveled trail along a restored wetland. Wildlife habitats like this are allowing endangered and threatened species to return to our communities. Spending time in such an area can help children learn that we are all part of an interconnected circle of life.

Chapter 8
Rain Garden Maintenance

"In an age when man has forgotten his origins and is blind even to his most essential needs for survival, water along with other resources has become the victim of his indifference."

Rachel Carson

A new rain garden is lovely. Plants are small, neat, and orderly and the bed is weed free. Everything is as it should be. To keep it that way will take some effort. For the first two years conscientious maintenance is critical to the future success of any garden. Remember, as plants become established, your rain garden should eventually require much less time and effort. At first the new plants will need special care. Since they have been selected for their ability to thrive in high moisture conditions, help them establish a strong root system by keeping soil evenly moist for the first few weeks. Their root systems need to penetrate and spread through the soil to form a web of life that will allow the plants to grow strong and help them to out-compete weeds in the future. At first they will require supplemental watering—about an inch a week— when there is not enough rainfall to keep soil moist. After the first three months gradually cut back on watering.

Young plants will need to be watched over for insect or animal predation. Make it a habit to carefully check the garden several times a week. This is a good activity in which to engage children. Frequent observation will help you notice problems such as wilting or excessive insect

Native and exotic plants combine to create exciting combinations.

damage in time to take remedial action. A few holes in leaves are not cause for worry, but if substantial portions of plants are disappearing, you will need to take preventive measures. Try to locate the culprit so you can describe it and consult your local extension service for advice on control.

Even in a suburban neighborhood, deer or rabbits may be tempted to sample the new plants. Early intervention will help prevent them from forming a long-term habit of visiting your garden. A strong spray from a nozzle controlled by a motion detector is very effective. You can also use repellant sprays or granules to discourage animals. If there are deer in your area, they are particularly destructive to young trees and woody shrubs. In the fall when bucks are scraping the velvet from their antlers, they may completely destroy young woody plants. Sturdy stakes with wire mesh fencing surrounding the trunks will discourage this activity. Wire mesh can also be laid flat on the ground around the garden. Deer will not walk on the mesh. Repellents can be used as well, but they need to be reapplied with some frequency.

Weeds are a major challenge until the plants become large enough to shade the soil and compete effectively for water and nutrients. The rain garden will always require a bit of weed control to remain healthy and attractive. For the first year, weeding should take place every two weeks or more often. Weeds should be pulled while they are small seedlings. If they are allowed to grow large they will disturb the roots of desirable plants when you pull them. The longer they remain in the soil the more rootlets, stolons, corms, and possibly even seeds they produce, making it harder to eradicate them completely. To prevent re-growth, remove all parts of weeds including leaves, stems, and roots. Take them out of the garden and compost or destroy them. This will result in a significant reduction in second year weeding. If you have planned well and kept the garden weeded until it's well established, an occasional monitoring and clean up will control weed growth in future years.

A large scale, low maintenance planting of perennial sunflowers and cup plant.

Mulching is a matter of some disagreement. There are those who advocate mulching and those who believe it to be a detrimental practice. I believe that mulching with organic material is beneficial to most plants. An established rain garden will mulch itself to some extent by dropping leaves and stalks to cover the soil surface. You don't need to lift a finger if it suits the style of your garden and your tolerance for some disorder. My feeling is that that organic material is very valuable to the health of the garden, but I don't enjoy the unkempt appearance. I rake up the surface litter and cut back stalks and grasses and run them through a shredder along with leaves raked off the lawn. This makes excellent mulch for the rain garden, adding nutrients and the soil improving benefits of organic mulch. It's cost free and it can be shredded right where you want to spread it, saving time and effort.

If neither of these solutions works for you then, by all means mulch with shredded hardwood bark. I do not recommend shredded wood mulches, especially those with added dyes. It seems to me that adding these dyes is defeating one of the purposes of the rain garden, that of filtering impurities out of the environment. Brightly colored mulches detract from the natural beauty of a garden and wood harbors termites. An annual application of two to three inches of mulch will help to keep moisture levels constant and block many weeds from germinating, both of which help desirable plants grow at maximum rates.

Pea gravel comes in several shades to complement any garden scheme.

Recycled glass is a colorful and permanent addition to the rain garden. *Credit ASG Glass*

For a permanent mulch or a garden path consider pea gravel or builder's sand as paving material. A layer of gravel, not more than 1 inch deep will give some of the benefits of an organic mulch, although it will not add nutrients to the soil. The gravel layer retains moisture and discourages many weeds. For a path, a thin layer of pea gravel can be spread over landscape fabric. Stone mulches and paths will need to be freshened after 5 to 10 years, depending on traffic.

After the first few heavy storms, check for washouts along the drainage channels or the edges of your rain garden. These can be stabilized with sod or large rocks. It may take a bit of re-grading if water is rushing over an area with sufficient velocity to cause serious erosion. Swales should be shallow enough to prevent this by spreading runoff over a wide surface. For the first two years continue to watch for wash outs and erosion and rework the grades until they are stabilized.

If you wish to add some exuberant color to your rain garden consider another permanent mulch material—recycled glass. Glass comes in a rainbow of colors and can be used as a garden feature or as a mulch material. Since it is a recycled product it is environmentally sensible. The bold look of glass should be used with care.

After a growing season it is often necessary to reevaluate the planting and make a few modifications.

In the first two years you will probably make some adjustments as you see how plantings grow and develop. By year three the garden should be pleasing to the eye and to the environment. It is well established and ready to maintain itself with just a little help from you. A monthly monitoring will help you keep the garden free of damaging insects and weeds. Don't forget to photograph each step along the way. It's fun to look back and see your garden progress from a mulched bed with small plants to a fully functioning ecosystem.

The contrast between smooth
mowed lawn and profuse
plantings creates a pleasing
picture while improving the
environment. Notice a haze of
water vapor above the trees.
Evapo-transpiration is recycling
moisture from soil to clouds
where it can gather and return
to earth as rain.

Conservation Guidelines for Garden Watering

• Keep the soil evenly moist for the first two weeks after planting

• Water weekly for the first three months. Water bi-weekly for the next three months

• Water when plants show the first signs of drying-leaves become pale or show signs of wilting.

• Water if there is an extended drought during the first two years after planting.

• Gradually decrease supplemental watering to encourage deep root penetration and strong plants.

• Supplemental watering should be unnecessary after the first two years.

• Use a rain gauge to measure the quantity of water your sprinkler applies.

• Never leave a sprinkler running until water runs off the area.

• Use shower, bath, or dishwashing water to water plants. The reservoir of your dehumidifier is an excellent source of water.

• Select from plants with low water requirements.

A rustic bench encourages you to spend time relaxing and getting to know your garden. This garden is an example of Xeroscaping. **(See chapter 9)**

Chapter 9
Conserving Water Every Day

"I have left almost to the last the magic of water, an element which owing to its changefulness of form and mood and colour and to the vast range of its effects is ever the principal source of landscape beauty, and has like music a mysterious influence over the mind."
Sir George Sitwell (*On the Making of Gardens*)

There are many ways to conserve water and improve our environment for the present and for future generations. We often look to government and environmental groups for the "Big Fix." In reality it is a thousand small everyday acts that make the world a better place. Now that you are aware of water problems and some of the solutions, you will most likely find other ways to conserve water and restore natural processes in your daily routines. A rain garden is one way you can help. Here are several others.

Water is a valuable element in the landscape as well as home and industry. We cannot survive without it. By conserving water now we will help to insure clean, clear water in plentiful supply in the future.

Pervious Paving for Walks, Driveways and Terraces: New paving materials have been developed to allow water to infiltrate through them. One of the early products to be introduced was grass pavers. These are cast concrete blocks with openings molded into them. The blocks are laid on a bed of builders sand and filled with topsoil. Grass seed is sown over them. As turf develops the concrete base protects root systems from light foot and vehicular traffic while allowing water to infiltrate. A lush green lawn can develop where it would have been worn away and killed by compaction of soil from traffic.

Asphalt paving materials have been developed to allow water infiltration. This material is not as strong as standard asphalt paving so it is not appropriate for extremely heavy traffic such as loaded tractor trailers, but it is useful for paths and light traffic areas such as car parks. The landscape architects of Land Studies, Inc. combine areas of permeable asphalt in parking lots where traffic is lightest and standard asphalt paving to bear the heaviest traffic.

New water permeable products are being introduced every day. Many of them are very attractive and long lasting. Some pervious materials are as old as the gardening tradition. For low traffic areas such as secondary walks and residential terraces, loose aggregate, such as pea gravel, is an excellent paving choice. The attractive texture and crunch underfoot are very appealing. The soft grays of Pennsylvania River Jacks are very popular. Red tipple stone is a good choice for added color. Those who have visited gardens in Europe or Great Britain have seen the durable charm of loose aggregate paving.

Instead of concrete surfaces, paving stones can be set into a builders sand base with topsoil brushed into the spaces between stones. Grass or herbs, such as thyme, may be grown in the spaces to keep weeds to a minimum while allowing water to infiltrate to the soil below.

Green roofs: With so much of the land covered by rooftops and pavement, some degree of flooding has become a frequent occurrence in urban places. Another problem caused by un-green surfaces is urban heat islands. Instead of absorbing sunlight and cooling the earth through evapo-transpiration, rooftops, roadways, and parking lots contribute to the buildup of searing heat. Urban areas are typically 10 degrees hotter than rural land. Roofs typically encompass almost 50 percent of the impermeable, heat reflecting surfaces. By covering rooftops with plants, many of the advantages of undeveloped land are restored. These plantings are known as "Living Roofs," "Garden Roofs," or most commonly as "Green Roofs."

Rooftop plantings of low maintenance Sedums, Sempervivums, and other hardy plants, conserve water by slowing the rate of runoff. They dramatically cut heat reflection and create pleasant green vistas. These roofs are widely accepted in industrial construction. They reduce cooling costs by as much as 40 percent, absorb carbon dioxide from the atmosphere, and reduce air currents caused by heat reflection from traditional roof surfaces. On a multi-level building, green roofs can provide uplifting green views from windows and rooftop gardens create pleasant outdoor areas for employees to gather. In some cities, new commercial construction requires green roofing. The City of Chicago has demonstrated its commitment to improving the environment by green roofing its city hall. There is an excellent website with all the details at www.chicagogreenroofs.com

The first green roofs were designed for large flat roofs, but new anchoring systems have been developed for planting on slanted roofs. They are becoming more widely accepted in residential construction as a result of these new products. Green roofs are virtually maintenance free and they are beautiful. For more information see *Green Roofs, Ecological Design and Construction* from Schiffer Publishing. Also see www.greenroofs.org or www.greenroofs.com. If you are planning on building a new house or commercial structure, consider the many advantages of a green roof.

Reforestation: Tree planting is one of the most significant ways of contributing to a healthy hydrologic cycle. Trees, shrubs, and herbaceous plants help to hold soil moisture, renew clouds for rainfall, cool the atmosphere in summer, and purify the air we breath. A tree that is planted today improves the environment far into the future.

Every acre of trees removes as much as 5 tons of carbon from the atmosphere in a year. Get behind tree planting programs in your community. It is also important to care for trees that are already growing. Observe the trees in your yard and along your street. If they aren't thriving, find out why and remedy the situation as best you can. They will pay you back in cooling, shade, clean air, and a more beautiful environment.

Use Water Wisely Every Day: There are many ways to conserve water on a daily basis. Following the garden watering guidelines in Chapter 8 is a good place to start. Use gray water (water from washing dishes, clothing, or bathing) to water your garden. Collect rainwater by placing rain barrels beneath downspouts. Use that water to wash cars, dogs, water plants, and for any use except drinking and cooking.

Minimize water waste in household maintenance. Wash only full loads of clothes and dishes and take showers instead of baths. Turn off the water while you brush your teeth. When you think about it there are many, many ways to conserve water in the home and garden. Small efforts on the part of each of us will have significant impact. In addition we can influence family and friends by our good example. Go to www.lcra.org/water/save/tips for more information.

An example of impervious paving. Runoff from roof and paving has no place to go. For an environmentally friendly solution, water could be piped from this hard paved area into a rain garden elsewhere on the property. When too much of the land is covered with impervious surfaces the hydrologic cycle is interrupted. Water shortages, floods, and drought occur more frequently.

A terrace with pea gravel paving allows water to percolate through the soil into groundwater. This type of paving allows for firm support for furniture and walking while addressing the issue of water conservation.

Composting: Yard waste and food scraps (excluding meat and fish) can be composted to produce a wonderful fertilizer and soil amendment for your garden. It also removes material from the waste stream, both landfills and sewage treatment in the case of garbage disposal users. Soil that is amended or mulched with compost retains moisture and requires less supplemental watering to maintain plant health.

There are several ways of composting. Garden supply stores sell a variety of composters that are unobtrusive in a suburban or urban setting. A compost bin can be as simple as low fenced area where garden litter and food waste can be layered and turned occasionally. Saving food scraps and adding to compost may seem strange at first. Many of us have been taught that food waste belongs in the garbage bin. However, once the habit is formed it becomes second nature. A friend of mine even collects lunch-time leftovers from his office and adds them to his compost pile. Compost has amazing power to keep plants healthy and growing. It almost seems magical in its ability to improve soil texture and moisture holding capacity and plant health. Some municipalities offer low cost composters and rain barrels or offer incentives to households that use them. For composting instructions go to www.journeytoforever.org.

Xeroscaping: Many plants have evolved in dry habitats. They will thrive in our gardens without supplemental watering. There is a huge palette of colorful plants suited to every region of the country. Sedums and Sempervivens are the most well known, but many herbs such as lavender, rosemary, sage, and dianthus fall into this category. Common characteristics of plants that tolerate dryness are thick succulent, leathery or waxy leaves that store water, often with a blue or gray color. Many plants from Mediterranean and dessert regions tolerate extreme dryness. These plants are not suitable for the rain garden, but they are useful for other beds in the low impact, sustainable garden.

By developing xeroscape gardens you contribute to environmental preservation by using less water and fewer resources to maintain plantings while you surround yourself with all the beauty you expect from a garden. Xeroscaping has many advantages for those who find common gardening chores physically challenging since much less maintenance is required.

A dry garden such as this can be very attractive and low maintenance.

Encourage and support municipal efforts to conserve water and prevent flooding. Municipal authorities respond to pressure from the community. Talk up the advantages of investing in water conservation and flood control through community rain gardens, flood plain restoration, reforestation, wetlands conservation, green roofs, and environmentally sound conservation schemes. There are powerful interest groups lobbying against environmental conservation investments. Governments will only act if there is a clear mandate from those of us who are concerned about the environment of today and tomorrow.

The pebble mulch helps reduce
weeding, retains soil moisture,
and cools the soil to benefit root
growth. Tamarisk, the small tree,
is a lovely feathery focal point
for this colorful planting.

Lavender is among many traditional Mediterranean plants that thrive with little or no supplemental watering. The gravel mulch allows surfaces to dry quickly and prevents stalks from contacting disease, especially during the winter months.

Chapter 10
Looking Toward Tomorrow

"When the well's dry, we know the worth of water."
Benjamin Franklin , Poor Richard's Almanac, 1746

Protecting and conserving our environment can easily become part of our daily routine. By recycling materials, composting organic waste and conserving energy whenever possible, we make a significant contribution to the world of our children and grandchildren. Managing storm water with a rain garden is an important measure that can be taken to preserve our water resources.

As you enjoy the seasonal pleasures of your rain garden—the flowers in spring, butterflies in summer, swaying grasses and colorful foliage in fall and birds feeding on seed heads over winter—it is satisfying to know you are doing your part to leave a healthier planet for future generations. When it comes to our fresh water resources, every drop counts.

Rain Garden Websites

www.mmsd.com/raingardens/index.cfm Lake Michigan Rain Gardens Initiative

www.whiteclay.org Site of the White Clay Creek National Wild & Scenic Rivers Program.

www. Raingardens.org Raingardens of West Michigan

Dof.virginia.gov/rft/rain-gardens.shmtl Virginia Department of Forestry

www.consciouschoice.com The Journal of Ecology and Natural Living

prairierivers.org/pipermail Illinois rivers coordinating council

www.rainkc.com 10,000Rain Gardens

www.dnr.state.wi.us/org/water/wm/npswww.raingardennetwork Wisconsin Department of Natural Resources

Raingardens.org/Marywood.php- Rain Gardens of Western Michigan

www.waterconserve.info A water conservation portal

www.chicagogreenroofs.com Information about Green and Garden Roofing systems in and around Chicago.

Water quotes throughout this book were drawn from the following websites:

www.gardendigest.com/water

www.gmd4.org/quotes

Glossary of Terms

Aquifer: an underground reservoir of water held in water bearing rock, sand gravel, or clay. Water is extracted from these reservoirs for human consumption.

Arable land: land that can be used for growing crops.

Bio-retention basin: landscaped depressions or shallow basins used to slow storm water runoff. Storm water is directed to the basin and then percolates through the soil where it is treated by a number of physical and biological processes. The water then infiltrates soils to recharge groundwater reserves

Bio-diversity: the mass of species that are interdependent in an established ecosystem. A wealth of biodiversity is one way of measuring the health of an ecosystem.

Bog garden: an artificially established and maintained wetland.

Condensation: the process by which water vapor is converted from a gas to a liquid.

Composting: a process by which bacteria, in the presence of oxygen and moisture, break down material to its basic components such as nutrients, water, and humus.

Desertification: the loss of productive land to desert as a result of environmental and human impact; most likely to occur in arid climates as a result of slash and burn agriculture and clearing of forests and grasslands.

Erosion: displacement of soil by the action of rushing water or wind.

Evaporation: conversion of water from a liquid to a gas or vapor. It is the way water moves from bodies of water and soil surfaces to atmospheric moisture, which then condenses and returns to earth as precipitation.

Evapo-transpiration: total water vapor released by the action of evaporation and transpiration from plants

Grey water: any water that has been used in the home, except water from toilets, is called grey water. Dish, shower, sink, and laundry water comprise 50-80 percent of residential "waste" water. This may be recycled for other purposes, especially landscape irrigation. (oasisdesign.net/greywater)

Hydrologic cycle: The circulation and conservation of earth's water. All life on earth is dependent upon this system.

Impermeable: not allowing liquids to pass through.

Impervious: not allowing entrance or passage. A surface such as a roof or driveway that does not allow water to pass through is an impervious surface.

Infill development: older structures, such as shopping centers or factory buildings, are refitted for modern uses. This is a significant conservation measure for land and materials.

Land subsidence: lowering of surface elevation from changes that take place underground such as pumping of ground water. The resulting sinkholes have been known to destabilize roads and buildings.

Non-Point Pollution: pollution from several sources that is picked up by water as it flows over the landscape.

Precipitation: moisture in any form falling to the earth as part of the hydrologic cycle. Precipitation occurs when atmospheric conditions are such that cloud particles become too heavy and fall to earth as rain, snow, sleet, or hail.

Percolation: filtering of fluids as they run through porous materials. The time it takes for a measured volume of water to completely disapate into the soil is the percolation rate.

Riparian: occuring on the interface between land and a body of water. Vegetation growing in the frequently saturated soils of river margins are called riparian plant communities. These plants would be good choices for a rain garden.

Riparian Management System: practices that reduce the physical impact of human activities and development on stream banks with the goal of reducing the input of nutrients and other pollutants. Buffer plantings are an example of a simple riparian management system.

Silting of streams: particulate matter is washed into streams by surface runoff, especially when vegetation is stripped and earth is bare. Streams beds may be blocked, resulting in flooding, fish and wildlife kill, and ecological imbalance.

Sinkhole: a natural depression or hole in the surface topography caused by the removing soil, bedrock, or both, by water. Sinkholes may vary in size from less than a meter to several hundred meters both in diameter and depth, and they may be formed gradually or suddenly.

Sustainable garden: A sustainable garden is one that will persist over time without the application of chemical fertilizers and pesticides and supplemental watering. Gardening practices such as composting, mulching, and careful plant selection minimize the need for negative practices.

Transpiration: The release of water vapor into the atmosphere by leaves and grasses. This is an important contributor to the hydrologic cycle that supports life on earth.

Wetland: Those areas that are inundated or saturated by surface or ground water at a frequency and duration sufficient to support vegetation typically adapted for life in saturated soil conditions. Wetlands are a very important part of the ecosystem in that they host considerable biodiversity and play a role in cleansing water resources. They generally include swamps, marshes, bogs, and similar areas.

Wet mesic soils: Water moves through these soils slowly enough to keep it wet for significant periods. These soils may become very dry at times. Plants indicated for this soil type would thrive in a rain garden.

Plant Sources

I have listed only mail order nurseries. I recommend using local retailers of native plants, trees and shrubs whenever possible.

Prairie Moon Nursery
32115 Prairie Lane
Winona, MN 55987
Toll Free: 866-417-8156
Phone: 507-452-1362
www.prairiemoon.com

Easywildflowers,
PO Box 522
Willow Springs, MO. 65793
Phone: 417-469-2611
www.easywildflowers.com

AmericanMeadow
223 Avenue D, Ste. 30
Williston, VT 05495
Phone: 877-309-7333
www.AmericanMeadows.com

High Country Garden
2902 Rufina Street
Santa Fe New Mexico 87507
Phone: 800-925-9387
www.highcountrygardens.com

Mail-Order Natives
P. O. Box 9366
Lee, FL 32059
Phone: 850-973-6830
www.mailordernatives.com

Tripple Brook Farm
37 Middle Road
Southampton, MA 01073
Phone: (413) 527-4626
www.tripplebrookfarm.com

White Oak Nursery
810 W. Washington St.
Geneva New York, 14456
Phone: 315-789-3509
Jengel53@rochester.rr.com

Sunlight Gardens
174 Golden Lane
Andersonville, TN 37705
Phone: 800-272-7396
www.Sunlightgardens.com

Woodlanders, Inc.
1128 Colleton Avenue
Aiken, SC 29801
Phone:(803) 648-7522
www.woodlanders.net

Design and Consultation

Land Studies
315 North Street
Lititz, PA 17453
Phone: 717-627-4440
www.landstudies.com

David Edgar Associates
740 Penllyn Road
Bluebell Pike
Blue Bell, PA 19422
Phone:610-584-5941
www.seddesignstudio.com

Wallace Associates Inc
P.O. Box 40
Kennett Square, PA 19348
Phone: 610-444-6161
www.wallacelandscape.com

Craig R. Stark
Landscape Designer/C.E.O.
Ecoscapes Sustainable Landscaping
Phone: 612-965-0848
www.ecoscapes1.com

Garden Rain Landscaping
Menlo Park, CA 94025
Phone: 650-224-2661

Kevin Robert Perry
Nevue Ngan Associates
1006 SE Grand Avenue, Suite 250
Portland, Oregon 97214
Phone: 503.239.0600
email: sedg@nevuegan.com

Judith Tabor
AmeriStone Farms, Inc.
28702 S State Route T
Garden City, MO 64747
Phone: 816-773-6301
AmeriStoneFarms@aol.com

Plant References

Dirr, Michael; *Hardy Trees and Shrubs: An Illustrated Encyclopedia*; Oregon; Timber Press, Inc; 1997

Rice, Graham & Kurt Bluemel; *Encyclopedia of Perennials*: New York; DK Publishing Inc; 2006

J. Robert Smith & Beatrice Scheer Smith; *The Prairie Garden: 70 Native Plants You Can Grow in Town or Country*, University of Wisconsin Press; 1980

Burrell, C. Colston; *A Gardener's Encyclopedia of Wildflowers: An Organic Guide to Choosing and Growing over 150 Beautiful Wildflowers*, Rodale Press; 1997

Reading List

Darke, Rick; *The American Woodland Garden*; Oregon; Timber Press; 2002

Diamond, Jared; *Collapse: How Societies Choose to Fail or Succeed*; Viking Penguin, 2005

Druse, Ken; *The Natural Garden*; New York; Clarkson N. Potter, Inc; 1992

Dunnett, Nigel & Andy Clayden; *Rain Gardens: Managing Water Sustainably in the Garden and Designed Landscape*, Timber Press, 2007

Jen Green, Wendy (editor), Mike Gordon (illustrator); *Why Should I Save Water?*; Barron's Educational Series, Incorporated; 2005

Kingsbury, Joel; *The New Perennial Garden*; New York; Henry Holt and Company; 1996

Kingsbury, Joel; *Natural Gardening in Small Spaces*; Oregon; Timber Press; 1996

Oudolf, Piet & Henk Gerritsen; *Planting the Natural Garden*; Oregon; Timber Press; 2003 (English edition)

Pearce, Fred; *When the Rivers Run Dry: Water – The Defining Crisis of the Twenty-first Century*; Beacon Press; March 2007

van Sweden, James; *Gardening with Nature*; New York; Random House; 1997, 2003

van Sweden, James; *Bold Romantic Gardens*; Australia; Florilegium; 1998

Index